HARDPRESS.NET

ISBN: 9781313930925

Published by:
HardPress Publishing
8345 NW 66TH ST #2561
MIAMI FL 33166-2626

Email: info@hardpress.net
Web: http://www.hardpress.net

UNIVERSITY OF CALIFORNIA
LOS ANGELES

EX LIBRIS

DEMOCRACY AND THE
DOG COLLAR

G. A. STUDDERT KENNEDY

'His publishers are well justified in advertising this author's writings as "the remarkable books by G. A. Studdert Kennedy."'—*Church Times.*

'There is a good deal of truth in the claim that the Rev. G. A. Studdert Kennedy is the most remarkable preacher of the day.'—*Church Family Newspaper.*

The Sorrows of God and other Poems
Food for the Fed-Up

This is a new volume of addresses by the author of 'Lies!' and of those two books 'The Hardest Part' and 'Rough Talks by a Padre,' which the critic in *The Weekly Dispatch* described as 'the most powerful books of their kind since Bunyan.'

Peace Rhymes of a Padre

'The straight talk to perfection.'—*Times.* 'Expressed with extraordinary force and outspokenness.'—*Bookman.*

Rough Rhymes of a Padre
More Rough Rhymes of a Padre

A THIRD EDITION has just been published at 2s. 6d. net paper of **LIES!**

'We doubt if any priest of our communion, or perhaps any communion at all, has such a gift of startling speech. . . . He speaks as the preaching friars may have spoken, in the language of the wayfaring man taken up into and fused with the eloquence of a master.'—*Church Times.*

Uniform with the above, but bound in cloth, 2s. 6d. net

The Hardest Part
Rough Talks by a Padre

HODDER & STOUGHTON, LTD., LONDON

DEMOCRACY AND THE DOG COLLAR

BY

G. A. STUDDERT KENNEDY

AUTHOR OF
"LIES!" "FOOD FOR THE FED UP," ETC.

HODDER AND STOUGHTON
LIMITED   LONDON
MCMXXI

TO
THE WORKING MEN OF BRITAIN
WHO WERE HER SOLDIERS ONCE

THIS BOOK IS DEDICATED

WITH AFFECTION AND RESPECT

THE FAITH AND THE HOPE

When through the whirl of wheels and engines humming,
Patient in power for the sons of men,
Peals like a trumpet promise of His coming,
Who in the clouds is pledged to come again ;

When through the night the furnace fires flaring,
Shooting out tongues of flame like leaping blood,
Speak to the heart of Love alive and daring,
Speak of the boundless energy of God ;

When in the depths the patient miner striving
Feels in his arms the vigour of the Lord,
Strikes for a kingdom and the King's arriving,
Holding his pick more splendid than the sword ;

When on the sweat of Labour and its sorrow,
Toiling in twilight flickering and dim,
Flames out the sunshine of the great to-morrow,
When all the world looks up because of Him :

Then will He come with meekness for His glory,
God in a workman's jacket as before,
Living again the eternal gospel story,
Sweeping the shavings from His workshop floor.

THE AUTHOR'S FOREWORD

This is not meant to be exhaustive, only suggestive. It is the result of many and many a friendly bout with pals among the workers. I make no pretence about it, the 'Dog Collar' is me (which is ungrammatical but expressive)—it is me talking as I believe for thousands of other dog collars, and doing my best to talk and think for Christ. If in passages I seem to be didactic and dogmatic, it is only because I want to be clear and plain spoken. I am still learning—you may say it is plain upon the face of it that I have much to learn. I am sure I shall learn much from my readers.

G. A. STUDDERT KENNEDY.

St. Paul's Vicarage,
Worcester, 1921.

CONTENTS

	PAGE
INTRODUCTION	1
THE CHURCH IS A DOG WITH A BAD NAME. HANG IT.	12
ORGANISED CHRISTIANITY IS A FAILURE	19
THE CHURCH IS NOT A MOVEMENT BUT A MOB	28
THE WORKER IS CONCERNED WITH FOOD, NOT FAITH	35
THE CHURCHES CANT ABOUT PEACE AND RECRUIT FOR WAR	44
THE WORKERS GET NOTHING THAT THEY DO NOT FIGHT FOR	51
THE WORKERS ARE OUT TO SMASH THE CAPITALIST SYSTEM	58
LABOUR HAS NO TIME FOR FINE ARGUMENTS. WE MEAN BUSINESS	67
CAPITALISM IS NOTHING BUT GREED, GRAB, AND PROFIT-MONGERING	77
WE WANT A SYSTEM BASED ON SERVICE, NOT SELFISHNESS	77
CAPITALISTS WILL FEAST WHILE WORKERS STARVE	87
THE CHURCHES PREACH SUBMISSION TO GOD'S WILL	92
WE MUST ABOLISH PRIVATE PROPERTY	100
CAPITALISTS ARE PAST PRAYING FOR	105

CONTENTS

	PAGE
THE IDOLATRY OF THRIFT	111
PROFIT-MONGERS AND WAGE SLAVES CANNOT BE GOOD MEN	121
LUXURY PLEADS POVERTY WITH ITS TONGUE IN ITS CHEEK	135
THE UNSELFISHNESS OF LABOUR	145
THE CHURCHES FUNK THE BREWERS	149
SO-CALLED RELIGIOUS EDUCATION WORSE THAN USELESS	162
THE WEAKNESS OF THE CHURCH HAS DESTROYED THE POWER OF THE CHRIST	173
THE UNIONS ARE BETTER BROTHERHOODS THAN THE CHURCHES	177
HUMANITY IS THE WORKERS' GOD: THEY DO NOT NEED A CHRIST	190
THE CHURCH WORSHIPS A NATIONAL GOD	205
THE WORKERS ARE BITTERLY DISAPPOINTED BY THE LEAGUE OF NATIONS	213
WANTED A REAL LABOUR LEADER	235
'SO LONG!' HOW LONG?	247

Introduction.

THE purpose of this book is to try and discover why the official relations between Organised Religion and Organised Labour are either non-existent or extremely bad. That this is the case there can be little doubt, for while there are individual Christian ministers of all denominations who live and work on the best possible terms with members of the Organised Labour Movement in their own town or district; and while there are in many congregations earnest and devoted Christians who are at the same time enthusiastic members of Trade Unions and energetic workers in the Labour cause, the two great organised bodies stand aloof from one another and there is no effective co-operation between them. Some would say, 'All the better, there ought not to be any; the less Christianity has to do with this or any other political movement the better. You cannot touch pitch without being defiled. Politics are blacker than any pitch, and Christianity cannot touch them without being defiled, degraded, and destroyed.'

Personally that appears to me to be a gospel of despair. The essence of Christianity is Christ, and the essence of Christ is that He *can* touch pitch without being defiled—that's what He came to do, and did. In the days of His flesh He handled pitch every day—dealt with it, moulded it, and turned it into gold, and then held out His spotless hands and called to a world defiled with sin, 'Come unto Me, and I will wash you white.' The doctrine that you cannot touch pitch without being defiled denies the gospel of the Incarnation, and damns the world to an inevitable hell. Something has got to touch the pitch of politics—something or somebody—or else there is no hope. It is a lie, and an extremely pernicious lie, to say that politics must remain dirty because they are dirty now. They can and must be redeemed, and as the Christian vision clears it becomes evident that to bear his part in redeeming the politics of his country is the only way in which a man can save his soul. No one can get to heaven on his own. There is only one way of getting through the gates. You have got to qualify as a builder, a builder of cities. You have got to be a politician, for a politician is a builder of the City of God. He is that now, whether he knows it or not. He may be a rotten builder, he may lay his stones all wrong and they may have to be taken down again; he may be a knave or he may be a fool, it's hard to know which is the worst, but a builder he has got to be.

God is the great politician. He is out to build a City—the new Jerusalem—and He has to work through subordinates and trust them. We are all His subordinates, some of us knaves and some of us fools (perhaps most of us rum mixtures of the two), but we are all He has got to work with and we all must play our part, we must all be politicians. That's the essence of Democracy, and with all my heart I believe that the City of God is to be a democracy. It would be tidier, more efficient, and less noisy if it were to be built as an autocracy or an oligarchy; but from what I can make out, God is not out for tidiness (if He is He has scored a failure so far, for this world is about the untidiest place I have ever been in—save us, what a muddle it all is!), or efficiency or silence, God is out for life. That is why He is a democrat, and would rather see a world of fat-headed, blundering, vicious fools that are free than a world of strong, silent super-men that are slaves. If you want to save your soul alive you have got to be a politician—a builder of the City of God—there is no other way. It is as politicians that we have to work out our own salvation with fear and trembling, and plenty of cause for it too, for it's about the most risky of all risky businesses. It's full of danger, therefore full of responsibility—and that's the essence of life, human life, for a human being is above all things morally responsible. It's no good, you can't wriggle out of it, you can't shut yourself up in a monastery and save your soul by prayers, cut off from the rest of the world. If you are doing your job in a monastery, you are only cutting your body off from the world that your soul may enter the more deeply into its sorrow and sin and play the larger part in its salvation. Even a monk must be a politician or else he cannot be a real working monk. He may of course be a purely self-centred recluse, but then he is not a Christian.

We cannot have any truck with this travesty of Christ's truth which would bid His servants save their souls and leave their brothers to be damned. Christianity has to do with politics, in fact it is politics—the politics of God. But you say, 'Oh yes, I know all about that. Of course Christianity has to do with politics in the wider sense, but surely it has nothing to do with party politics; it cannot take sides, and therefore cannot co-operate with the Labour Party.' That is true, but Organised Labour is something more than a political party, it is a wider, bigger thing and has more behind it. It is a world-wide movement of humanity, by far the most impressive and challenging movement of modern history. It enters into the world not merely as a new political party but as a new political power, fraught with enormous possibilities of good and evil. It has behind it the aspirations, hopes, and dreams of untold millions of dumbly suffering people who only find a voice through it ; and though often its speech betrays its great heart, and its actions betray it more deeply still, the heart is there and the voice will speak more and more clearly as the head becomes more intelligent and better educated.

I am not a member of the Labour Party, nor do I propose to become one, but for that very reason I feel the less inclined to confuse the movement with the party. They are two entirely different things. I am just as little disposed to identify the Labour Party with the Labour Movement as I am disposed to identify the Anglican Communion with the Christian Church, and to suppose that a man cannot be saved unless he attends matins. I am a member of the Christian Church, and believe that with all its faults and failings it is by far the greatest of all human movements in the history of the world. Here are two great human movements—the Labour Movement and the Christian Church—and I feel that the world's salvation and the building of the City of God depends upon there being some understanding and co-operation between them. The bother at present is that the understanding seems to be mainly a misunderstanding. While they have very largely, as far as this world is concerned, the same hopes, the same dreams, and the same purposes they stand aloof from one another, and their efforts tend to overlap and cut

THE DOG COLLAR

one another out. The object of this book is to discover, as far as possible, the reasons for that misunderstanding, and to see what steps (if any) can be taken to put it right.

I think we shall probably get down most directly to business if we take two imaginary people and suppose that a Conference has been fixed between them. The representative of Organised Christianity will have to be, I fear, a purely imaginary person, for to find any real person to represent the broken and divided Church of to-day would be a literal impossibility, and thereby hangs a tale, and a peculiarly sad one. The representative of Organised Labour need not be purely imaginary, but he must be largely founded on fact, for the labour world is not nearly so united as it seems. You can picture the actors in the scene as you please. You can clothe the Christian in a cardinal's robes, a dog collar and a frock-coat, or a white tie, a moustache, and benignant smile just as you please. You can picture the Labour representative as a bushy-whiskered, blood-thirsty Bolshevist with two bombs and a copy of the *Workers' Dreadnought* in one hand and a red flag in the other, but if you do you will probably be wrong; it will probably be nearer the truth if you draw a composite portrait of Mr. Hodges, Mr. Thomas, and Mr. Clynes, with a dash of Mr. Williams and George Lansbury — but only a dash (Organised Labour really takes even its *Daily Herald* with a pinch of salt)—but do that as you please.

Mr. Organised Labour sits at a table and Mr. Organised Christianity comes in at the door to keep an appointment with him. It is not for nothing that Christianity is represented as coming to Labour, that is generally the case nowadays. Labour is generally the Mountain and Christianity Mohammed. Some people think that is contemptible, I think it is merely Christian. It is for the Christian to hold out his hand first; he ought not to be afraid of humility, Christ was not. If the world takes that for weakness so much the worse for the world, it's an old mistake after all. 'He was despised and rejected of men,' and is to-day.

The Dean of St. Paul's says that Organised Christianity in these matters is always on one side — the winning side — and is nothing but a creaking weather-cock. I suspect, like many another of his outspoken sayings, this is rather more outspoken than true. There is truth in the wind that moves the weather-cock, and it is better to creak under the blast of truth than to croak because there is something the matter with your inside and you won't move. And I am afraid that is what is the matter with the Dean. I fear that it would break his heart if he found that he was popular, which as a matter of fact he is. He is quite one of the most amusing and entertaining speakers of to-day.

I am going to assume, at any rate, that some sort of effective co-operation between these two great human movements would be an advantage to mankind, and on the basis of that assumption let us get down to business.

The Church is a dog with a bad name. Hang it.

Mr. O. C. (*kicking off*). ' I have come to discuss with you the reasons why our two movements, which, in their aims and objects, have so much in common, are in practice so very far apart and fail so completely to establish a really effective co-operation. Now why do you stand aloof from us ? '

Mr. O. L. 'Well, you see, old son, you've got a shocking reputation, your record is rotten bad. During the whole of the last century, when the workers were up against it with their backs against the wall, you Christian people did little or nothing to help and the devil of a lot to hinder. You pretty consistently supported the classes against the masses. You ranted about heaven hereafter to people who lived in hell here. You supported the forces of reaction against the forces of revolt, and many of your foremost leaders were the avowed enemies of the people. You held on to your fat bishoprics and your comfortable livings, and on the strength of a good dinner preached about the blessings of poverty to people with empty bellies. You pocketed the profits of a rotten system and persecuted the prophets of the brotherhood of man. Give a dog a bad name and you might as well hang it. You've got a rotten bad name with the workers of the world, and so far as they are concerned you can go hang—and that's that. Mind you, I'm talking as a Labour man, not as an individual, and I'm talking to you as an Institution, not as a man—in fact, I'm talking to your collar and not to you; take it off and we are pals.'

MR. O. C. 'I'll keep it on, thank you. It often hurts the back of my neck, but some jolly fine men have worn it and I am not ashamed of it. It stands for, and in the main I believe it always has stood for, a white world. But I agree with you and plead guilty! It's a bad business; Church history surely gives one the creeps at times, it's so terribly hard on Christ. But you know we have publicly confessed and repented of our failure in the nineteenth century at least three times in the last twelve years—once in the report of the Pan-Anglican Congress of 1908, again in the Archbishop's Report on Industrial Affairs in 1916, and now more fully and completely in the Lambeth Conference Report of 1920. We are sorry—very sorry. When I read of some of the horrors which were permitted to pass unchallenged in those days I go hot with shame, and I do not mind telling you that I have shed some tears over books like Hammond's *Town Labourer.* It was damnable. But that is the past. What is the good of kicking me for the sins of my grandfather? It doesn't help us any to allow the past to dominate the present, and rake up the dead to damn the souls of the living, does it? There is a whole lot to do still, and we are out to get it done. Why can't we do it together, your movement and mine?'

Mr. O. L. 'Oh, we don't mind you

doing what you like, but we do not think you are likely to cut much ice. You never have done in the past. You have only been on the winning side once it was sure to win, and that's what you seem to be after now. I don't want to doubt your honesty, but you're a bit like the copper who always comes up when the row is over to see what it's all about—aren't you now? Don't you think there is always a kind of likeness between a bishop and a policeman?'

Mr. O. C. 'But this beastly row is not over—not by a long chalk; you do not think we are out of the wood yet, do you? Good Lord, go to Halifax or Hull. Besides, although I allow that what you said about the Church in the time of good Queen Victoria was a true bill, I think you draw a long bow about the total indifference of Christians to the evils of that day. If you would read a book like Mr. Raven's *Christian Socialism* I think you would admit that all the historians of the Labour movement without exception have done a great deal less than justice to the work of such men as F. D. Maurice, Charles Kingsley, J. H. Ludlow, Tom Hughes, Charles Neale, and the other Christian Socialists. How many of your people know anything about them at all? And yet, mind you, they were real pioneers, and practical pioneers at that. They did much more lasting and effective work than men like Feargus O'Connor and his crew, who bawled out red revolution and put the wind up decent people who might have been won to the workers' side. They played a real part in influencing the public opinion of that day and providing the workers with expert legal advice, which they urgently needed, besides fighting their battles in Parliament.

B

'The fact is that a just estimate of the work done by Christians of those days to better the conditions of the working classes can only be arrived at after a careful, critical, and sympathetic examination of their history; and I say that the study of history in your Labour colleges is neither careful, critical, nor sympathetic, but hopelessly biased, lopsided, and shallow. You are out to teach your people how to support your case, not how to find the truth. Your teachers serve out red spectacles before they start their classes, and that gives a hopelessly artificial colouring to the whole thing. All spectacles are bad, but red ones are the very devil.

'Honestly, I am worried about this education of the workers. It seems to be aimed much more at making passionate revolutionaries than clear thinkers, good citizens, and sane men, and I find the results of it everywhere in working people's minds, and especially in their complete and dismal ignorance of what they owe to the great Christian reformers of the last century.'

Organised Christianity is a Failure.

Mr. O. L. 'Well, I'm not prepared to admit all that. If our teaching of history is bad yours is worse. Our history does live, yours is dead. It is better to study the life of the people, even with red spectacles on, than to learn lists of English kings by heart and probe into the domestic affairs of a common vulgar blackguard like Henry VIII. When I left school I knew nothing—absolutely nothing—about the past of the English peasant, and the manner of his life in other days. I was just stuffed up with the wretched intrigues and wars into which his rotten rulers plunged him. The real tragedy and the real glory of history never dawned on me at all until I read it as the story of the workman's martyrdom. I have never been to a university, but I doubt if they are much better. If there is a mote in my eye, how about the blessed clothes-prop sticking out of yours? And anyway, our quarrel has never been with individual Christians, nor are we concerned to deny that there have been good Christian men and women who have nobly championed our cause. Our quarrel is not with them any more than mine is with you —our quarrel is with the Institution, with organised Christianity; it is that which seems to us to be a hopeless failure. There are many of us who would call ourselves Christians, and have a tremendous admiration for the character of Jesus of Nazareth, but we simply can't see how you square His gospel with the practice and position of the churches of to-day. It is the organised body which we say has failed.'

Mr. O. C. 'Yes, I understand that, and I agree. Organised Christianity is a failure, but then *organised anything is a failure*. Christianity is a life, and you cannot really organise life in its fulness, it always tends to break its body and reform it into a more perfect expression of its real soul. It is not only organised *religious* life that fails and is always crying out for reformation; organised political life fails, and is always crying out for reformation. That is the necessity that lies behind political change. An organisation that was not a failure could never hope ultimately to succeed—it would be dead. Christ has always been greater than His Church, and always must be, until His Church becomes the new Jerusalem and the Kingdom of God. Your own organisation is a failure. I should not bother about it if it were a complete success, because I should know it was dead, but it is a living and growing thing, continually changing its outward form and practical policy, and obviously greater than any of its manifestations. And it is just the same way with the Church—it is a failure, and has been, because it has always been an organism more or less alive. As that acute and learned writer John Theodore Merz says in his *A Fragment of the Human Mind,* " The whole of modern history has been influenced by the dominating force of this great structure of Christian thought and Christian life. It was subjected to the most virulent attacks in the earlier centuries of our era, and to relentless criticism in more recent times. It has not fallen but steadily gained ground. It has been misused and perverted as an instrument for gaining and extending purely worldly interests—it has never lost its inherent and fundamental spirituality. . . . It has been denounced as antiquated and superseded, it has always reasserted itself again." That is the wonder of Christ—He comes again, keeps on coming again.

'I am perfectly well aware that I cannot plead the work and attitude of the Christian Socialists as representative of the Church of their day, but I would contend that it was prophetic of the Church of this day, and that the prophecy has largely been fulfilled. I say that the Lambeth Conference Report does prove that the official body of the Church of England, at any rate, has arrived at the point to which the greatest churchman of the last century, Dr. F. D. Maurice, gave his life to lead it, and I would urge upon you that it is absurd to let the dead hand of a wretched past choke the breath out of a living present, and prevent an alliance between

Christ and the workers of the world. I admit that the Church has been a failure—is a failure still—but I maintain that it is alive, and that its very life is the cause of its failure.'

Mr. O. L. 'Well, there may be some truth in that, and I'm not saying there is not, but you know I do not think that your church, or any other church, has really got as far as you suppose. There are still thousands of your people who keep their business and their politics for week days, and their religion for Sundays only. Your church may not be so much a class church as it was, but your churches are almost all class churches—some for the rich, some for the poor, and most for the middle classes. Your preachers are still largely class preachers, with one gospel for the poor, another for the rich. Slum parsons are sometimes Socialists, but you do not find many of them in the West End, do you? You see, you depend for your funds on rich people, and you cannot afford to offend them. We are not blaming you, we only state facts. You are all mixed up with this rotten system. The very life of your organisation depends upon it. We cannot expect you to commit suicide, and that's why we do not look to you for very much help. It is the money that puts the tin hat on it as usual.'

Mr. O. C. 'There's a lot of truth in that, but it's not all true. You have got your red spectacles on, and you are looking at things cock-eyed. You are making the usual class-war assumption that a man cannot be a member of what is called the "upper class" and have any sympathy with Labour and its aspirations. You are assuming that a man's outlook is of necessity determined solely by his economic position, and I tell you that assumption is not true. I tell you there is a strong movement in the heart of the Church, arising from and commanding the support of men of all classes who have the most intense and real sympathy with the higher aspirations and hopes of Labour men, who are convinced that the old world and the old systems are worn out and are crying for radical and complete reformation. These men want to make the Church the Church of the people. The Church of the people, mind you, not the Church of your class, because we do not recognise class distinction in any form. We hold that the collier is as good as the king, but also that the king is just as good as the collier, providing that he does his job. Christ's Church must find room for all, and must treat all alike; kings and colliers, poets and plumbers, labourers with hand and with brain, all alike are God's children and workers in God's world. *We want a world in which social position is based solely upon social service, and in which there are no idlers, no gorgeous coloured drones.* We want that and want it very badly—some of us want it more than anything else in the world—and we do not believe we can get it while such an enormous body of the men of England stand aloof from religion and the religious motive. Honestly, it is not that we want to capture the Labour Movement for the Church; we believe that we have something to give Labour as Labour has something to give us. God made the Church for the people, and not the people for the Church. We are willing that the Church should perish, nay we are anxious that *the Church as it is* should perish, if only the people are saved. Frankly we are not anxious about the Church; it needs no protection but its own eternal truth; it never has had any real protection but its truth, all other Church defences are useless and built on sand. We want the people to find the truth, and that is all we do want.'

The Church is not a Movement but a Mob.

Mr. O. L. 'Well, I personally am willing to take your word for it, but mind you all our people are not—not by a long chalk. They suspect you, they think you are out for your own ends, they do not trust you, and you will have a job to make them trust you—and they have reason for their mistrust. When you talk like that you are only really talking for yourself, or at any rate a small section of what you call the Church. Yes, I know you can plead that the bishops are behind you, but the bishops do not make the Church any more than the leaders make the Labour Party. You may have the bishops behind you, but you have not

THE DOG COLLAR 29

got the rank and file of Christians. That is where the shoe really pinches. You are not a Church, you are a chaos of churches. It is not as though you came as a unit seeking co-operation with another unit; you have no unity, you are all split up, you are not an army, you are a mob. And what I want you to grip and hold on to tight is that the great need of the Labour Movement is solidarity—a closer and closer solidarity. We know because we have learned by bitter experience that we stand or fall together. Split the Labour Movement and you kill it. Now if we started co-operation with you we should split, we should be bound to split. To start with, there would come the big split. You see, some of our members believe in God and some don't; some believe in the Christian standard of morality—I mean the one man one wife and strict divorce laws standard — but there are some comrades in this country and more on the continent who don't believe in that standard at all, who hold that it is an impossible and ridiculous ideal which creates a lot of unnecessary misery and vice. Please don't misunderstand me. I don't in the least mean what I hear one of your Tory Lords declared was the truth, that it is our policy to nationalise women. That is an infernal lie, and English Labour stands clean opposed to any such idea. The point is that we have no policy on these matters. As we are at present, it does not matter what a man believes in, he can please himself, and still remain a good comrade and a loyal member of the workers' brotherhood. We are not concerned with a man's morals or his beliefs, and therefore we can comprehend all. But once we touch you there would come the split and our members would be divided in their loyalties, and that we cannot afford. And there is more of it too, because there would be not only the big split, there would be a whole bunch of little splits. We would be like a battalion on Church parade split up into sections—Church of England on the left, Roman Catholics on the right, Baptists, Wesleyans, and Presbyterians in the centre, and all the fancy religions in the rear. How can you get solidarity out of a mob like that? I can't see the Pope and the Archbishop of Canterbury and General Booth waving the workers' red flag and singing Labour songs to a Gregorian chant accompanied by the Salvation Army band and a big drum, can you? Don't you think that before you come asking for any unity with us you had better start and unite among yourselves? You want a bottle of your own physic.'

Mr. O. C. 'Yes, I agree. But to take that last matter first—I mean the matter of the little splits. Once more I would plead that the Church has already recognised and repented of what she calls her " unhappy divisions "; she has recognised that they are wrong and she has started to put an end to them. We are out after a united Church. It is not easy because these splits have long histories behind them. It is not easy, but we are out to do it. And that is one place where you could help us. You see, these questions will never be finally solved by ecclesiastics and ecclesiastical assemblies. In the end they must be solved by the people themselves. If the workers' movement could be brought into touch with the churches, they would bring us down to tin tacks, make us sit up and take notice of our main job—which is turning out good men and women. At present we discuss the difference between a presbyter and a priest, or the comparative merits of a chasuble and a frock-coat as a proper Eucharist vestment, and whether bishops are of the *esse* or the *bene esse* or the *male esse* of the Church. We cannot get any further with questions like that. They don't want solving, they want blowing up, literally blowing up out of the world of convention into the world of reality, then they would solve themselves. We want blowing up, and you are the blokes to light the fuse, and that is one reason why we want you. And besides I say that, divided as we are on theological and ecclesiastical questions, there is a very real unity among us upon these social questions. We are all of us out for the same big principles—the Fatherhood of God, the Brotherhood of Man, and the infinite value of the individual soul. We are out to declare that we must either apply these principles to every department of our lives, individual, national, and international, or be prepared to perish. And surely these principles are, or ought to be, the basis of your movement too, and so some sort of co-operation with us — even in our present divided state—ought not to be impossible.

'And then with regard to the other matter of the great split. Here we come to the real crux, because on this business we cannot compromise one blessed inch. Our moral standard and the main outlines of our faith are fixed, firm, and unalterable. We are convinced that those men who do not believe in God, in the other world, and in the Christian ideal of marriage are as great a danger to your movement as they are to the world at large. Great and powerful as your movement appears to be to-day, we do not believe that it has any future before it unless it takes over, and adopts as its own, the moral and spiritual ideals of Jesus Christ. We are convinced that it would in the end pay you hand over fist to risk the big split and go for a thoroughly Christian Labour Movement; do that, and we believe the world is yours.'

The Worker is concerned with Food, not Faith.

MR. O. L. ' Well, for the life of me I cannot see why we should bother our heads about the morals or beliefs of our members. After all, when you get down to tin tacks, the problems we are out to solve are economic problems. The workers' question is a bread and butter question. We are first of all concerned with men's bodies, and we are pretty certain that if you look after their bodies their souls will look after themselves. What we are really out to secure is that there is a proper standard of life for the people. We are quite content to leave the cure of their souls to those who know, or think they know, how to cure them. We are really out to see that they are properly fed and housed, and that they have their fair share of the things that make life worth living, and I don't see from Adam what God and the world to come and people's moral standards have to do with it. These are questions of pounds, shillings, and pence. We want a new economic theory on which to base a new economic practice—we are out to smash the present system.'

Mr. O. C. '"Smash the system"—blow it up—that's it—that's where you start talking through your Sunday hat, right straight through your Sunday hat—and if you go on talking in that way and thinking in that way you are going to land us in the devil of a mess, and so far from getting a higher standard of life for your people that sort of talk is going to bring us to starvation. You seem to think, and your speakers are always implying, that you can get an improved standard of life by fighting for it or by continually striking for it. You are always reducing, or trying to reduce, what are in fact extremely complicated questions to a ridiculous and artificial simplicity in order that you may get a good war cry out of them. It is of course much easier to get men to fight than it is to get them to think, and although I believe your leaders know—they must know—that there is nothing to be got by fighting for it, there is the constant temptation that comes to men who have to hold audiences and lead men in masses, to play down to the body they want to move, and your papers and your speakers are always doing it. You talk as if what you call the Capitalist System was really a system, a thing which having been deliberately made can be deliberately destroyed. You seem to imagine that on a certain date a number of clever devils —sort of super-devils whom you call Capitalists—sat round a table and formed an elaborate and carefully constructed plan to exploit Labour and steal profits. The secret of this plan presumably has been passed down from father to son, and the heirs of these infernal tricksters still sit in high places and live upon the swag of that first epoch-making burglary. All that is needed now is that the workers should band themselves together, force the blighters to disgorge, and then sit down on golden stools and drink the wine of life for ever like the children of the gods. Of course that's a caricature, but it's a just caricature.

'"The inevitable outcome of democracy is . . . the recovery of what John Stuart Mill calls 'the enormous share which the possessors of industry are able to take of the total produce,'" says Mr. Sidney Webb. It is that "enormous share" that bothers you. That is what you are out for. You are out to fight the super-devils and get away with the swag. As one of your speakers put it the other day in the peroration of his speech, "We who have so long been the lean and hungry spectators or hardly driven waiters at the feast of life are now going to burst into the banquet hall, turn these swinish gourmands out, and sit down ourselves to eat." I shall never forget that speech. I was carried away by its eloquence, and by the picture of universal peace and contentment which the speaker drew — a picture which represented exactly what I wanted myself. I remember when it was over that I went out of the hall in which the meeting had been held and stood on the steps outside, lost in a brown study and asking myself questions. Was it really as simple as all that? Could it be solved that way? Was I going the wrong way about helping the poor? Ought I, instead of holding up before them the ideals of Jesus Christ, and seeking to make them fine and God-fearing men and women, ought I to be leading them out to the great battle against the greedy and conscienceless Capitalist? Ought I to be filling them with hatred and bitterness against their oppressors, crying to them, " Workers of the world, unite and strike a blow for what is yours "? I found myself longing that it might be so, it seemed such a simple programme, so much easier and infinitely more exciting than my own or Christ's. But as the effect of the speaker's eloquence began to wear off

I began to remember some solid facts, the truth began to dawn, and just at that moment three factory girls passed by with their arms linked—bonny girls they were, I remember, and rather prettily dressed—and they were singing in harmony:—

> '"I am blowing bubbles,
> Pretty bubbles in the air,
> They fly so high
> Up to the sky
> Then like my dreams they fade and die.
> I am blowing bubbles,
> Pretty bubbles in the air,"

and I got a lump in my throat because I seemed to see millions of people like them, the toiling millions of the world, led by men like you, all sitting in the moonlight, gazing into this land of perfect peace and plenty, and singing in a chorus like the sound of many waters, " We are blowing bubbles, bubbles in the air." It was the great host of the bamboozled and deceived.

'I see that picture again and again when I am reading the *Daily Herald* or listening to some of your speakers, and I am free to confess that at times it makes me bitterly angry. It is not that the vast majority of workers really believe all this tale—an enormous number of them have far too much common sense—but it hangs around them as a general atmosphere, it produces a vague unreasoning and unreasonable discontent, which destroys at once their happiness and their power to settle down and work. Instinctively they turn to politics rather than to industry as the source of wealth, and that is perfectly hopeless. You cannot make a country rich on wind and words. I am perfectly aware that by juggling with figures and statistics it is possible to make out that there is enough for all as things are now, but it is necessary to play the most extraordinary tricks with the figures and use the oddest economic definitions before that can be done; and when you have finished, all that you have really proved is that there are three kinds of liars—liars, damned liars, and statisticians. One thing is plumb dead certain, and that is that you cannot get a higher standard of life without hard work, and to encourage any idea that you can do so is to tell the biggest lie and the cruellest that you can tell a man to-day.

'The very first thing that any true friend of Labour has got to make quite clear to the workers to-day is that there is just as little to be got out of industrial war in the long run as there is out of international war, and that little is considerably less than nothing. If we have learned anything from the past five years of hell, it surely ought to be that war never gets anything or anywhere. It is in every case a disaster which it is the bounden duty of every sane thinking person to hold out against till the very last ditch. It is and it never can be anything but a pure and unmitigated disaster, and my great grouse against that sort of easy talk about " smashing " the system is that it gives men the impression that they can secure the millennium by knocking down a policeman, and it is that lie which, like some kind of deadly mist, is blinding the eyes of the working people to the things that really belong unto their peace.'

The Churches cant about Peace and recruit for War.

Mr. O. L. 'Oh yes, I know all that sort of talk. You parsons and your Church have always been alternately recruiting sergeants for international war and strike-breakers in industrial disputes. You are all against war when the workers fight to win their own, and all for it when the Capitalist classes drive the workers out like sheep to be killed in the shambles of international war fought to secure their interests. During this last bust up your pulpits rang with patriotic sermons and talk of the Great Sacrifice, but now that it is over and the workers have come back to a land that it needs heroes to live in, you suddenly turn pacifist. Truth of the matter is that you are not honest with yourselves, you are all of one class, Oxford, Cambridge, and a Theological College; and nice old ladies who live on fat dividends support your charities and supply you with afternoon tea. Your sympathy with the workers is only veneer, and your real quality comes out when there has to be a fight, and then you are all for peace. All that you mean by the application of Christian principles to the solution of industrial problems is that the wicked workers must not fight, they must work hard like good industrious people and be content with their wages. I have no patience with you. What's the good of this conversation anyhow? It won't land us anywhere or do us any good. You went to the war yourself, I know you did; did you ever say a word against it? If you had been true to your creed you would have been a "Conchie," but you hadn't the guts for that. You are not true to your creed and you don't really believe it. The Labour Party are better Christians than you are, they have always been opposed to war.'

Mr. O. C. 'Yes, I thought we should get a bit hot on this business, but for heaven's sake let's keep calm. If we once start to fight we shall cease to think, and then it's all up with us as far as doing any good is concerned.

This question of force and the right and wrong use of it is just about the most bewildering and difficult of any with which we have to deal. I say that you have got to start off with the fundamental conviction that the appeal to force never does any actual good and is always a disaster; but that is not the same thing as saying that it is never necessary—it may be. Disasters do happen in this world, and war may be forced upon us. If anybody proposed to take away from the workers the right to strike, I should oppose them tooth and nail—I mean by argument and reason. A strike may be absolutely necessary, but when it is, it must be recognised as a necessary *evil*, which must not be allowed to last a moment longer than can possibly be helped; and the same with war.

'When I went into my study in August 1914 to decide what I as a Christian minister was to do about this business, I went in to one of those horrible hours of my life. I believed then as I believe now, only not so clearly or completely, that war was a disaster. I did not believe it quite so clearly and completely then because I, like many others, had a kind of hope and faith that war would have a purifying and uplifting effect upon the character of the nation as a whole, and that out of this valley of the shadow of death we should come a nobler and a purer people. I know now that this was a delusion, and that war is not merely waste of life, but is degrading and brutalising to the spirit of man. But I decided to play my part in the war rather than protest against it, *because I believed that, disastrous as it was, it was forced upon us, and that if we refused to accept the challenge a greater and more awful disaster would fall upon us—not merely upon us as a nation, but upon the world as a whole.* I am not sure now that that is true, but I was sure then, and it was on those grounds that I decided. I believe that it was on those grounds that the Church as a whole decided, and I suppose that it was upon those grounds that millions of your members decided too ; for British Labour went solid enough for war whatever you may say.

'Now, those are the only grounds upon which it can ever be right to support a strike or a war, only when you believe, and have good grounds for your belief, first that it is absolutely forced upon you, and secondly (though, as a matter of fact, it amounts to the same thing) that a more terrible and morally impossible disaster, a greater wrong, will follow your refusal to support it. I acknowledge that this right attitude is a difficult one to maintain, because if you are to lead people to war, industrial or international, you must give them a clear call and keep their spirits high, and that is hard to do unless you can hold in front of them the prospect not merely of avoiding an evil, but of gaining some positive good. Half our trouble arises out of that fact, because we only won the war by holding up before the people the prospect not merely of avoiding disaster but of winning a new and better world. People are always skitting at Lloyd George for promising us a land fit for heroes to live in, but it is very doubtful whether without some such promises the heroes would have been forthcoming as they were. We were really fighting to avoid disaster, but were forced to pretend that we should win real good. It was eye-wash and self-deception, but it was necessary if we were to win. We deceived ourselves then, but we must not continue the deception now; and so the chief task which falls upon leaders in these days is to keep clearly before themselves, and clearly before their people, the truth that *it is not possible to win any positive good out of war whether industrial or international*, and that therefore it must be always the very last resort. It is just here that I think your Labour leadership is at fault. You are continually falling into the old trap, and consciously or unconsciously telling your people the old lie—the lie which has lured the nations again and again to plunge themselves into seas of horror—the lie that the Kingdom of Heaven can be won by force.'

The Workers get nothing that they do not fight for.

MR. O. L. 'I don't know anything about the Kingdom of Heaven, and I'm not concerned with it. What I'm after is the kingdom of earth. You are playing your old trick and going up into the sky, and if we are to continue this discussion to any purpose, you've got to keep your boot soles flat on the ground. And when it comes to the earth I think a great deal of that is pure bilge. Isn't it a fact that whatever advance the workers have made, and whatever improvement has been brought about in their standard of living, has been won by fighting for it? You answer me this: do you think that the masters are going to pay the workers a ha'penny more than they can actually be forced to pay by threat of strike? If we hadn't struck shouldn't we be where we were in the fifties, aye and later on than that, when an agricultural labourer came home and turned up ten bob and a couple of swedes at the end of the week? Facts are facts, and it is a fact that whatever we have we have because we've fought for it—now isn't it?'

Mr. O. C. 'No, I say that it is not. It is not a fact but a fable. I say that that doctrine is not supported by a real understanding of history. The improvement of the standard of living has come from two main causes :—

1. The increase in the productive power of industry following on the release of the energy stored in coal and the invention of machinery; and
2. The slow and gradual change that has taken place in public opinion with regard to the rights of man.

I maintain that the power by which the Labour Movement has done its best and most powerful work is the power which lies in the essential righteousness of its cause, the appeal which it has made to the conscience of men.

It is by that power that it has succeeded in breaking down the forces opposed to it. It has been able to advance because it has continuously undermined the moral defences of its enemies; it has put a traitor into the opposite camp, and the name of that traitor is CONSCIENCE. Public opinion has been so changed that a present-day employer literally cannot look upon his workpeople in the way his grandfather did. Labour has been able to make its voice heard, in the main, not by mere force of numbers or strength of combination, but because it has been able to convince people that the voice of Labour was the voice of justice. It was certainly no mere strength of combination or brute force of numbers that repealed the Combination Laws in 1824, or secured the passing of the Industrial and Provident Societies Act of 1852, and it is largely by virtue of those two acts that the

Trade Union Movement has any legal standing. They were in some respects the most important pieces of social legislation of the century, and the most substantial triumphs that the workers won. It is one of those things that sounds so honest and downright that it ought to be true, but as a matter of fact is false, to say that the workers never got anything they did not fight for. It does not bear the test of historical investigation. Many of the most fruitful victories that have been won for the working people have been won because they were able to convince some of the best people in the land that their cause was the cause of right. The history of the Labour Movement as a whole makes it clear that the best work that was done for it in the nineteenth century was done for it by men who were not of the working class, but had been convinced that their cause was a righteous one, and that still remains true. The greatest enemy that Labour has to-day is the ignorantly enthusiastic demagogue of the labouring class who continually preaches class war as the only way to decent conditions and a fuller life. The best friends of Labour to-day are the men of goodwill *in every class of society*, who are convinced that it is wrong to sweat and oppress the working people, and that somehow or other the problem of poverty has got to be solved.

'I say that it is by the power of righteousness that the Labour Movement has advanced, and I say that it is by the power of righteousness that the Labour Movement must and will advance. All that force or actual strength of combination has achieved is to make the voice of Labour and its righteous claims more clearly and distinctly heard. When the movement has relied mainly on righteousness it has been able to secure advance, when it has relied mainly on force it has merely stiffened the backs of its enemies and retarded advance. And although the history of the last few years may not seem to bear this out, I believe that in the long run it will prove to be the case, and that the only advances that Labour will be able to consolidate and hold are those that it has been able to convince the community are just and right. Meanwhile it is impossible to estimate the damage that has been done to the cause of the worker and to his actual standard of life by pursuance of the war policy.

'I would plead most earnestly with you to read history more carefully, and with a more discerning judgment, in that light, and not to accept as an axiom that needs no proof the statement that Labour has secured nothing but what it has fought for. I tell you that you have advanced and will advance much more because you are right than because you are powerful.'

The Workers are out to smash the Capitalist System.

Mr. O. L. 'Well, old son, from my present standpoint I should say that a great deal of that appears to me to be moonshine, though there may perhaps be more in it than I am inclined to think. But surely you would allow that what we have to do is to change the system—it is the system that is wrong, isn't it ?—and until we have smashed that we can never really get any forrarder. Of course I agree that strikes do a certain amount of damage to the worker as well as to the capitalist, but if strikes are necessary in order to alter the system—if, in fact, war is actually forced upon the working classes, as I believe it is and you admit that it may be, then are we not justified in prosecuting it and organising for it with all our might and main? If you want peace must you not at any rate prepare for war? That's a sound old Tory doctrine and ought to find an echo in your soul, which, if you will pardon me saying it, is an essentially bourgeois soul; it is really impossible for you to understand the point of view of the proletariat.'

Mr. O. C. 'Oh my holy Aunt! I knew we should come to the bourgeois and the proletariat sooner or later. It is extraordinary how impossible it is to get rid of the ghost of Karl Marx. *Das Kapital* is really the Bible of the working classes; they swear by it and don't read it, and could not understand it if they did. I am fed up with the whole performance. I believe that old gentleman ought to be buried. He was not really a prophet, he was only a disease. He lived in an age when men worshipped their own intellects, and he positively grovelled before his. That old lie about preparing for war does not find any echo in my soul, it rouses nothing but the most violent antagonism, and I spring at once to a complete denial. It is a lie—in the quite strict and theological meaning of the word it is a damned lie. If there is anything that the history of Europe from 1870 to 1914 has done, it is to damn that old lie for ever and ever, amen and amen. No, I say that if the workers really want to attain to the things that belong unto their peace, let them seek peace and ensue it by every means within their power. You cannot smash the system—the system is not a system, it's a growth; it never was deliberately made, it grew — grew out of human nature. The world grew into it and it has jolly well got to grow out of it, and that's the only way it ever will get out of it. It is not a thing that you can smash, it is like trying to smash a lump of india-rubber, or snap a piece of chewing-gum—it's the wrong method.'

Mr. O. L. 'There is a lot of sense in that, but don't you admit that we have got to have a complete revolution, whether you bring it about by force or by gradual evolution?'

Mr. O. C. 'Excuse me interrupting, but those are not really alternatives, you can only bring it about by evolution. Revolution of the bloody description could only be a regrettable incident in the necessary evolution—and when it was finished the evolution would have to begin once more from a point somewhere farther back than that to which it had previously attained. Evolution is the only method, but it need not of necessity be slow, that depends upon the character of the people who work it.'

Mr. O. L. 'The character of the people! What in thunder has that got to do with it? If you said it depends upon their wits and upon their education, I could understand you. You are always dragging in character, but after all what does it matter? These questions are economic questions—you are always trying to make them religious questions, and I cannot see what economic questions have really got to do with religion. The Capitalist system is the root evil, and it has got to go. Under the present system a man cannot be decent if he wants to. More than half the crime which you call the "wickedness of this wicked world" is due to the system under which we live, and the only way to cure it is to change the system.'

Mr. O. C. 'Look here, you have got that system on the brain. It's clouding you, I tell you, and putting you in a mist. Come out of it and think. The question we have to decide is—Do men make systems or systems make men, or is it a bit of both? If it's absolutely true that it's systems that make men, and not men that make systems, it's all up with us—we cannot do anything—what will be will be, and we cannot help it. When you make that statement you are down in the depths of determinism, and determinism is not so much a real intellectual attitude as a moral disease. I know perfectly well that an intellectual case can be made out for it, but there is something much stronger than intellect which is opposed to it—the instinct of freedom, and the instinct of freedom is the meaning of manhood.

'You always land up against this

question when you start talking with a Marxian Socialist. I remember some time ago one of them came to me and argued for an hour and a half—or rather discoursed—to prove to me that the more deeply I thought the more I should become convinced that I was the pure product of heredity and environment, and that my every action was determined absolutely and before I did it—that I was, in fact, the result, and not in any sense the creator, of the system under which I lived.

'His position was :—

> '"After years of thinking,
> I know just what I am;
> I am a thing that runs on rails,
> Not even a bus, but a tram."

He discoursed extremely cleverly; but at last I could stand it no longer, and I jumped to my feet, kicked a table, a glass of water, and a box of cigarettes into a corner, and said 'Damn' three times very distinctly. My friend was perturbed, and remarked that that was not argument but abuse. I replied, "No, it is the final argument and the only one; it is the assertion of the instinct of freedom, and against that rock of instinct seas of pure cold reason have broken and will break in vain." That is where your astounding blindness and inconsistency comes in. Can't you see that when you get on to the determinist tack you are selling the whole show into the hands of your opponents? Determinism as a creed is destructive of all human values, the very values you want to preserve. It is the creed upon which the whole of what you call the present system is founded. The extreme Capitalist will tell you that our whole life is ordered and determined for us by the constant action of what he calls economic law —iron and inexorable economic law.

We cannot alter it or change it, rebellion is useless—it acts with the same inexorable impartiality as gravity. That was the philosophy of nineteenth-century Capitalism, and it was also the philosophy of nineteenth-century Marxism. Marx was not really original, he was very much the slave of his time. Marxism and extreme Capitalism have exactly the same philosophic basis—the same assumption underlies them both, viz. universal and inevitable economic determinism. Systems make men, not men systems. That is the creed that has divorced business and politics from morality—from all idea of right and wrong. Marxian Socialism and Manchester Capitalism are both morally diseased, and can only lead men to disaster. There are forces in human nature which instinctively rebel against both, all the forces which in history have issued in the fight for political freedom. The finer a man is the more intensely convinced he is that he is not merely an effect but a cause, not merely a thing that is made, but a person who is deliberately making. To ignore or neglect those instinctive forces is to court disaster, it is to try and work on an economic theory which has no psychological basis.'

Labour has no time for fine arguments. We mean business.

Mr. O. L. ' Look here, old son, you are getting too deep for me, half my time I don't know what the devil you are talking about. What do you mean by a psychological basis ? Are these questions of pounds, shillings, and pence, or are they not ? Is this a bread and butter question, or isn't it ? What have pounds, shillings, and pence got to do with psychology and the instinct of freedom and all those other jawbreakers ? I don't believe there's anything in all this tosh. The question is a much simpler one than you make out. The people want more grub, more leisure, and better conditions, and we have got to get them for them, and that's all there is to it.'

Mr. O. C. 'Now you are getting tired of thinking, that's what's the matter with you. And I tell you you must not, you have got to go on thinking even if it busts your old brain pan. These are bread and butter questions, but they are *human* bread and butter questions; they are questions of pounds, shillings, and pence, but they are questions of *human* pounds, shillings, and pence—*human* do you hear—have you got that through your head? And once you start to deal with human anything it ceases to be simple and becomes complex, because a human being is about the most complex piece of machinery that the Lord God ever made. He's a positive corker, he knocks a flying machine into a cocked hat, and if you start tinkering with him without understanding his complexities, like as not his propeller will start going like fury, and you will get a knock on the head that will give you instant relief from all your troubles—including toothache—for all eternity. That's where half the trouble comes in. As I have said before, you are always trying to make these things simple because you get tired of thinking, and they are not simple, I tell you they are complex. Pounds, shillings, and pence *have* got to do with psychology; they are pure matters of psychology because they are human pounds, shillings, and pence, and the most important element about a human being is his psychology—the working of his mind, the motives that govern his actions. Money has got no reality at all apart from the human mind and will—it is nothing but a conventional symbol of human activities and human desires and the motives that govern those activities and desires.

'Have you ever tried to plough through Professor Marshall's *Principles of Economics* ? If you did I bet you got tired of thinking then—I know I did—but mind you, it's a good book still. Now listen to what that dry but extremely sound old gentleman says on page 22 :—

'"Though it is true that 'money' or general purchasing power or 'command of material wealth' is the centre around which economic science clusters, this is so not because money or material wealth is regarded as the main aim of human effort, nor even as affording the main subject matter for the study of the economist, but because in this world of ours it is *the one convenient means of measuring human motive on a large scale.*"

'Money is the one convenient means

of measuring human motives on a large scale, and economic science is ultimately the science of human motives. That is why I keep dragging character in. I can't keep it out, because character is of the essence of the question, human character being the sum of human motives. I wonder if you've got that?'

Mr. O. L. 'I don't think I have, and I'm not sure you have either. Money is not the means of measuring motive, it's the means of buying grub.'

Mr. O. C. 'Yes it is, and what makes you want it?'

Mr. O. L. 'What makes me want what? What makes me want money? Why, grub of course. I want grub and my children want grub; I want money, because if I don't have it we'll have to go with empty bellies.'

Mr. O. C. 'Yes, well, that's the motive that moves you, that's the motive that makes you work, and money is the way that motive is measured. The amount you will give for a thing measures your hunger for it. Money measures the motive for work. But is grub the only thing you want?'

Mr. O. L. 'No, of course it's not. I want beer and tobacco and the picture-house and the theatre, and my wife wants Buckingham Palace, a carriage and pair, ten motor cars, and a new dress for every day of the week.'

Mr. O. C. 'And you want domestic peace, and so you work hard to get her what she wants, and your wages are a way of measuring the motive of the desire for domestic peace which moves you to work. Money is a way of measuring work, and behind work there has to be a motive that moves a man to work, and so money is the most convenient means of measuring human motive on a large scale.'

Mr. O. L. 'Well, I begin to see

daylight now. I think I understand what you mean.'

Mr. O. C. ' I thought we should get to it. Money does measure motives. The amount that you will give for a thing is one of the best ways of measuring how much you want it, and that is what money is for. It is the best rough measure of how much people want things, and how much inconvenience they will put up with to get them. But, supposing you get a large number of people, all obliged to live together, and there is only a certain amount of grub and beer and tobacco and all the rest of it, and they all want as much as they can get, and to take as little trouble as possible to get it, how do you think they will get on ? '

Mr. O. L. ' Well, I imagine they would be a rough house—something like Lord Carson addressing a Sinn Fein demonstration.'

Mr. O. C. 'Yes, and that's the struggle for existence, that's animal life, that's nature, and in that struggle the weak must go to the wall and the strong must take the lion's share. The ultimate appeal is to strength—it may be strength of body or it may be strength of mind, it may be cunning, craft, skill in deception; for those are often greater powers than purely physical strength. The great fact which we have to notice about the pure struggle for existence is that it has behind it only one motive power, only one driving force, and that is the desire of each individual to satisfy his own needs and his own wants. Your Marxian contends that human life always has been and always must be like that, because men always have been and always must be moved by the one motive, and the one motive only, the economic motive of self-interest. That is the essence of

Marxian Socialism and pure Capitalism alike. They postulate the same struggle for existence *as a necessity,* but look at it from different ends. They both believe in Economic Determinism, but look forward to a different issue finally. But the truth is that the struggle for existence among men has never been " pure " in that way—it has never had a single simple motive like that behind it. There is another motive which appears first, as Prince Kropatkin showed, among the higher animals, but finds its fullest development among man—the social motive, the desire to serve and to help. Human society in so far as it has ever existed at all has been based upon these two motives— the selfish and the social. The social motive takes its rise from the love of children, and then spreads outwards; the family becomes the clan, the clan the tribe, the tribe the nation; and at that point the development has been checked, but shows signs of proceeding further.

'There have been these two motives, the selfish and the social, working together through the greater part of human history. The perfection of society seems only to be possible when the social motive becomes as strong, if not stronger than the selfish one, and when the range of its action includes the entire human race. In other words, the purpose of human development appears to be that we may progressively transform the struggle for existence into a co-operative effort to build a human society, and the great means to that end is to strengthen, in every way that lies within our power, the social and unselfish motives of action, and extend their range as far as we possibly can.'

Capitalism is nothing but Greed, Grab, and Profit-mongering.

Mr. O. L. 'Yes, and that's exactly what the present system does not do. The present system is all based on one motive, there's nothing behind it but grab, grab, grab, there's nothing social in it, it all wants blowing up and a proper social system wants establishing—we always get back to that in the end. What is there behind Capitalism but greed, grab, and profit-mongering? Capitalism is the pure struggle for existence and nothing else.'

We want a System based on Service, not Selfishness.

Mr. O. C. 'Steady on now, that's not all true, although there is a great deal of truth in it, and you do your cause damage by raving when you ought to be thinking. It is not strictly true that there is nothing behind the present system but greed; the social motive is not dead, but there is a fear lest it is dying. I will grant you this, that pure Capitalism as it was preached and practised in the middle of the nineteenth century was very little more than a pure struggle for existence in which the weak were allowed very largely to go to the wall, and to be crushed out by starvation. It was a terrible system, because in theory and in practice it was based upon a single incentive, it was based entirely upon one motive of production—the motive of self-interest. It was assumed that there was only one reliable motive for work, viz. the hope of gain. It did not deny the presence of other motives and their action, but it did deny that they could ever be reliable or be taken into account in schemes for legislation and management. That is the basic assumption of pure Capitalism, and therein lies its most appalling danger, because, relying as it does only upon one motive, that one motive is the only one that it strengthens and calls into active exercise, and its tendency therefore is to stunt and deform human nature, by failing altogether to bring out or to educate the nobler side of man. But although it has undoubtedly succeeded in weakening the purely social motive of public service, it has not succeeded in killing it—it is still there, thank God, in both employers and employed. It is doubtful whether it could be killed, though there is unfortunately little doubt that through lack of exercise it can become so weak as to be quite unreliable and of no use as a basis for any sort of reform.

'It is the gradual weakening of the truly social motive that has been the really paralysing and destructive feature of industrialism. Left to itself it tends more and more to become a purely one-motive system. It comes to be assumed by practical men that there is only one secure basis for the political and industrial system, because there is only one reliable incentive to work, and that the incentive of selfishness disguised under the fine-sounding title of "enlightened self-interest." The present apparently absolute deadlock to which Capital and Labour have come is really a moral and spiritual deadlock, which is the inevitable result of a one-motive system, not a purely economic deadlock.'

Mr. O. L. 'Well, I kind of sense what you are driving at; but surely what we have got to do then is to alter the system, to change and reform it at once. If we have been relying too much on one motive only, and not calling out the motive of public service, isn't it time we started to do it, and isn't the best way to do it to start out and reform the management of industry from top to bottom and put it on another basis ?'

Mr. O. C. 'Yes, I think we have got to, but before we can even start to do that with any sort of safety, we must realise where we stand, we must realise that we cannot go on any longer upon one motive, and must create a demand for reform *upon moral grounds* —upon moral grounds mind you, and not merely on the ground that the present order does not give us all we want. It is true that there is already an enormous demand for reform, but the worst of it is that that demand has behind it so much of the *purely selfish motive,* and so little of the truly social one.

'There is between the two sides— between employers and employed—a bitterness and suspicion which arises from the fact that each assumes the other to be actuated by only the one motive of self-interest, and the cruel part of it is that the suspicion is so largely justified. It is useless to pretend that all the class selfishness is on one side only—it is on both; neither side is able to believe that the other has any really noble basis on which to found its case, and until we can assume some higher motive on both sides we are on the horns of an absolute dilemma, and are bound to come to a deadlock. It reminds me of the story that is told of a kindly and good-natured Yorkshireman who went into a public-house to enjoy a glass of beer and the pleasures of good fellowship. In the course of the evening a member of the company was called upon to sing a song, but was unable to find a pianist. The kindly and good-natured one volunteered. "I don't know that much 'bout pianer playin' tha' knows, but we mun just do our best," he said cheerfully. They started, and the results were dreadful. "Nay, lads," said our friend, "that sounds summat awful, like a lot o' cats what have got mixed up in a dog-fight. We mun start this ere song ower again." They started, and the result was worse. At last the pianist dropped his hands from the piano in despair, and scratching the back of his head said, "Nay, Bill, that caps owt. I've tried t' black 'uns and I've tried t' white uns, but by gum tha sings a'tween t' cracks."

'Of course that's a funny story. When I first heard it it caused me much joy, but the passage from comedy to tragedy is always a short one, and the very finest laughter always trembles on the edge of tears. The humour of the story arises from the paralysing effect of a *false dilemma*. There was a third way out: he could not see it, we do, and it makes us laugh. It makes us laugh in that case, because it does not matter much whether he gets out or not; but supposing it did matter, supposing it were of vital importance that he should get out, supposing his purpose were not the production of an accompaniment to an ale-house song, but the production of food and warmth and fulness of life for a great people or a world of peoples, then the paralysing effect of that false dilemma would no longer be comic but tragic—a matter no longer for laughter but for bitter tears.

'That is the situation precisely as it stands to-day. The leaders of Organised Labour have issued a manifesto in which they state emphatically that they are not going to permit any attack upon the standard of life of the people. Behind that defiant declaration there lies a fear, the old, old horror that has hung like a cloud over the lives of working people for centuries. I agree with you entirely, of course, that the standard of life is not merely a sordid and material thing, and Labour's challenge is not merely a sordid and material thing. The standard of life stands for fatter, brighter, jollier, and more intelligent children, it stands for the hope of fuller life. The determination to resist an attack upon the standard has much in it that is fine and noble, but it is all mixed up with selfishness, greed, and political ambition, all mixed up with the determination of men, not merely to get what they earn, but to get as much as they can. Well, that is one side of the dilemma—the white side so to speak. The other side has been clearly and dispassionately stated by the business economists. We regret it, they say, but unfortunately the standard of life is not a thing which we can fix. It cannot be fixed by Labour, it cannot be fixed by Capital, it cannot in the end be fixed by Government, it is finally fixed and determined for us by the action of economic law — iron and inexorable economic law, and to that law we must submit or face industrial ruin. It is all nonsense to talk of attack on or defence of the standard of life, no one is attacking it, it is no good trying to attack it, it is fixed by the laws of nature. That is the other side of the dilemma— the black side so to speak, and it is black because it means apparently that we must return to our slum statistics, every unit of whose thousands stands for a starved and stunted human life. It means, as a business man said to me, that the working classes have got to learn their lesson, and that until three men are looking for one man's job and a good many children are going to bed crying with hunger we shall never be right.'

Capitalists will feast while Workers starve.

Mr. O. L. ' Yes, damn them, that's exactly what they would say. They have got no bowels of compassion, they have got no humanity, they can't think of anything but profits. What do they care about slums and starvation ? They are all right with their servants, their dinners, and their holidays in Switzerland. But if that's what they are counting on, the starving of the working people into submission, they are counting their chickens before they are hatched. They have forgotten that Labour is no longer made up of a lot of worms that can be trodden on as they will. Labour is united and powerful, and the working people are not going to starve, they are going to fight, and we will tear their old, rotten system into pieces before we will starve. If we are going to be ruined they are going to be ruined too, and we will all go down together. But we are not going to starve while they feast, and our children are not going to tramp round with no boots while they ride in motor cars with fat bellies. That's the fight, and that's the fight in which the Church ought to be leading the forces of the down-trodden and oppressed. That's business, and business is the very devil himself. That's what makes me sick of all your talk about psychology and instinctive forces and all the rest of the bilge. It's a fight I tell you, and it's got to be fought out to a finish, and we've no time to waste on wind and words.'

Mr. O. C. 'Fight to a finish. Go down with your flag flying. Die in the last ditch. Boo-bunkum and nonsense. War cant, the essence of muddle-headed self-deception and lying. If I'm not sick of it. For the Lord's sake come off it. Dry up. Haven't we had four years of it—waving flags and beating drums and making blithering idiots of ourselves? You must not do it for the sake of the women and children and their standard of life, you must not do it. Our people will be eating red flags for dinner, breakfast, supper, and tea, because there isn't anything else, if you go on. Of course the man who said that was a fool. He was a blessed anachronism — fifty years behind the times. He was a bone-shaker bike in a motor show. He was trusting in weapons that were broken in his hands years ago. He was as woolly-headed as Karl Marx, or you thinking of the " Capitalist System " as a system—a fixed and static thing that cannot be changed, when it is changing every day. He was blind not only to the power of the workers' combinations, but to the radical change that has taken place in public opinion on these matters. It is not only you that are determined the people shall not starve—the community is determined on it—we could not stand it. But what you have to grasp is that this man is not the cynical cold-blooded devil you take him for. He is no more hard-hearted than you are. I know him, and I know he's not. He's as good a father and as good a husband, and a man with as kindly a heart as any man in England. It's not half as much his heart as his head that's weak. He believes in this economic law business. He's an economic determinist like you. He believes that we are in the grip of the false dilemma, and sees no way out. He believes what you believe or say you believe, that it's the system. The system governs men, controls their every action, and determines their standard of life.

He believes that we are the helpless victims of economic laws over which we have no control. He is just like you, you are both in one box, and you have both got to come out of it. It's an iron box, a cage, a trap—all determinism is. As long as you both continue to believe that lie the paralysis must continue, and we must all go down the slippery slope that ends in anarchy, disruption, and industrial decay. What you have got to realise is human freedom, moral freedom. The dilemma is not an economic dilemma at bottom—it is a moral one. It is the moral dilemma into which all one-motive systems are bound to work themselves in the end, and which leads to strikes and wars. Strikes and wars are not regrettable incidents in the working of purely selfish one-motive systems, they are of the essence of that working. Of course Marx was logical. He was a German, and all Germans are logical, and that is why they are often such silly fools. The logical conclusion of an economically determined society is that it should destroy itself by splitting into two vast but perfectly selfish combinations locked in a death struggle, and so finish, bust, and make general napoo of mankind. That is logic all right—but thank God it is not life. We can break clear of economic determinism and claim our moral freedom. We can make our systems, they need not make us. We can cease to be interest-determined, money-determined, profit-determined machines, and become *God-determined men.* That is the road out of the dilemma—the power of the moral motive through God.'

The Churches preach Submission to God's Will.

Mr. O. L. 'But don't you teach that God is at the back of all this ? Isn't that the whole trend of your religion? People must submit to the will of Almighty God. Doesn't He determine who shall be rich and who shall be poor?

> ' "The Rich man in his castle,
> The Poor man at his gate,
> God made them high or lowly
> And ordered their estate."

That's what I was taught, and to order myself lowly and reverently to my elders and betters, and be content in that state of life into which it had pleased God to call me. Isn't this supposed to be God's world, according to you—governed by God's laws? I can remember when my little brother died thirty years ago, died of diphtheria from a bad stink in our backyard—I can remember Mother telling Dad that it was God's will, and Dad saying, "God be damned, it's these blasted drains." That's when I first started to think about God really. I didn't think before that, I only swallowed what I was told. When I did start to think of Him, I thought Him out of the world soon enough, and thousands of other workers have done the same. One of the best fellows in our Union was a Baptist Sunday School Teacher once; but he got fed up with God. He worked a Sunday School in the slums of Birmingham, and as he said, if God made the slums of Birmingham he'd got no blinkin' use for God whatever. He got sick of teaching kiddies who lived in pigstyes to do God's will and be content. That's what has driven thousands of the best working men out of your churches—they can't believe in Almighty God, King of Kings and Lord of Lords and all the rest of it—nor can I. You say we have got to rise up and change the world, but how can we change the world if it's God's world? Isn't it all arranged by Providence? The Prime

THE DOG COLLAR 95

Minister was on the pious tack the other day in Parliament, and said that Providence had arranged that there should be poor pits and rich pits, and that therefore there must be poor miners and rich miners. That's religion, isn't it—God's will be done?'

MR. O. C. 'No, that's not religion. It is the oldest enemy of true religion. It is the enemy which all down the ages the religion of Christ has had to struggle with. You see, men are naturally fatalists. Fatalism is the philosophy of sloth. Naturally men never move until they are pushed. They say, "What will be will be, and I can't help it." What's the good of bothering? Sleep, slumber, snore—that is the natural tendency, and in a thousand different forms that law of death which avoids mental and moral effort crops up in human history. All the pessimist philosophies are just philosophies of sloth—elaborate justifications of jelly-backed despair—whereby men prove that they are fated to sleep on a muck-heap to avoid the trouble of shifting it. At its root that is what all determinism means—just sloth. Of course this oldest of all human errors wormed its way into the religion of Christ in the form of the powerful Providence. It put on its religious disguise, which is servile reverence and submission to the will of an unknown God. That is its oldest suit of clothes, and it wears well. The confusion in Christian teaching which has driven so many workers out of the churches is caused by the attempt to reconcile that law of death with Christ's law of eternal and ever fuller life, the attempt to follow Christ and yet avoid the cross of continual mental and moral struggle that following Him involves. Christ calls us to a patient and persistent strife with the limitations of the material world and the natural man. We must put off the old man, the slothful, lazy fatalist, who says what will be will be, and turns to sensual sleep, and we must constantly put on the new man, who rises in the power of God above the limitations of his lower nature, and presses forward earnestly to attain perfection. That strife is the essence of Christianity, but the natural man in Christians has always tried to avoid it, and the most popular refuge from it has always been the fatalistic creed—the blasphemous piety that ascribes both good and evil to the will of God, and cries over a cruel, dirty, and chaotic world, " Thy will be done." At times this old enemy has obscured the Christ and usurped the central place in religious teaching—it has done much to cripple Christ, but it has never killed Him. Still He calls men out to strive and hurl defiance at all fate, and still men hear His call. That is the call which comes to the workers to-day, and it is of urgent and paramount importance that they should hear it, that they should shake themselves free of this vile old error, and declare war on fate in every form, whether it be the blasphemous piety of the comfortable Christian or the pseudo-scientific, economic determinism of Karl Marx, that they should assert their moral manhood and their present power to do right, and strive for right by the help of God. If we continue to believe in economic fatalism and work upon one motive, we must continue to struggle over the product of industry, and in the struggle fritter away our power to produce, and that means ruin; for, however much there may be on the surface that seems to contradict it, our greatest economic need is still production.

'We must realise that God, Love, Co-operation, Unity, the Spirit, is the only real producer, the only real creative power. We must realise it, and we can. I want the miner to feel when he is down there in his pit that he is not merely working for his wage—working for Friday night—a wage slave—but that he is a Priest of God, a Priest of Love called by God to produce warmth and power for his brothers in the world. I want him to feel that he is as much a priest down there in the dark, filthy black and streaming with sweat, as I am a priest when I stand at the altar and plead for the wants of men. The coal black is as white as my white robes, and sweat is sacramental wine poured in service of God's world. He is the Right Honourable the Collier, one of the greatest and worthiest servants of the human race. I want him to feel that about himself, and I want other people to feel that about him. That's the Spirit, and that's the call that has in it power to destroy this dirty, muddled, ugly world, and build a city of God upon the ruins.'

We must abolish Private Property.

MR. O. L. ' Yes, that sounds all right, but you'll never get it home to our fellows, never in the world as long as the present system lasts. For why? Because we are not producing food and light and fuller life for God's children, as you would call it; we are producing bigger profits for a lot of thieves, we are producing royalties and filling up the pockets of a lot of men who never do a stroke of work or any act of service all their lives. The root of this problem is in private property. You will never get any further until you have abolished private property. What's the good of pleading poverty and talking to working men about its being wrong to get as much out of the poor community as they can by combination and by force while the community continues to pay large incomes to people who do nothing ? If a man has only a right to what he can honestly earn, then these people have no right to live, they ought to be put out of their misery. Your moral appeal is no good, and is bound to fall flat until you have abolished private property. When the workman can feel that he is working for the nation in a nationalised system of industry you can make any moral appeal you like with some hope of response, but until that happens you may as well keep your breath to cool your porridge.

'We must not continue to get all we can—the wicked workers must not—but what does the business man aim at ? Why, he aims at getting into an independent position, a position in which he will have no need to work and can leave his children so that they need not work, and he will combine and form trusts and combinations and rings, or adopt any other means to get there, so long as he gets there. The one thing he wants is to be independent and perfectly secure, free from the fear of want—aye, and free from the fear of work for ever—and that's all we want. We cannot attain to that sublime heaven really. What we can do is to shorten hours and raise wages. We cannot get everything for absolutely nothing, but we can get as much as we can for as little as we can, and in doing that we are acting upon the best business principles—combining to sell our labour in the dearest market we can find, as the business men combine to sell their capital in the dearest market they can find. It's no good talking to workers about the dignity of Labour when the main aim of all Capitalists is to attain the dignity of idleness.'

Mr. O. C. 'I agree with you all the road, that's just it. But the point we've got to realise is that two wrongs don't make one right, and that if we try and make them into right we drift inevitably down. Even now, under present conditions, it remains true that work is a vocation, and that the man who works at the production of necessaries is a priest of God and the servant of his fellow-men, and has a right to the respect of all for that reason, and therefore ought to pride himself on being respectable. There is no prouder title in the world, even under present conditions, than that of a "*working man.*" Because there are men trying to degrade labour and exalt idleness, looking at the world all cock-eyed, there is no reason why the working man should lower himself to their level—no final reason why even now the collier should not reckon himself as a king among men, and hold his head high, and do his level best. If he does that he can claim with tremendous force *on moral grounds* that these abuses of property should be abolished, and I believe that his claim will be honoured. The call is for working men to strike their way out of this viciously immoral circle, and assert in act and in word the dignity of Labour, making as a respectable and dignified body of men a united moral protest against the abuses of property. It is behind that protest that I believe the Christian Churches are ready to put themselves with all the power they possess, and I submit to you that that power is considerably greater than you suppose. We are making a strenuous effort to organise the Christian conscience on these matters and to make it vocal, and I believe that whatever the united Christian conscience of this country demands insistently it can finally obtain. But at present our greatest obstacle is the fact that as an organised body Labour stands aloof and suspicious, and will not join with us in this purely moral protest.'

Capitalists are past praying for.

Mr. O. L. 'We won't join because we don't believe it's any good. We believe that the other side are past praying for, and that they will hold on until the last ditch, and that if we do our best and deliver the goods all the moral protest business will collapse. We believe that the only thing that will drive property-holders and share-mongers into surrender is the prospect of national ruin, and we are not going to produce to bolster up a system which is rotten at the core. We are not going to produce until we get our fair share of the product. We will never be right until we have abolished private property.'

Mr. O. C. 'Yes, and it is because you believe that they are past praying for that you will never win them. Fight begets fight. You stiffen the backs of your opponents and throw away your greatest weapon when you talk like that. You spoil your case every time by going the whole hog, and crying out that you are going to abolish not only the abuse but the use of things perfectly good in themselves. When you talk about abolishing private property you put the wind up every decent man who has worked hard and saved a bit, and wants to keep it for his old age and for his children. When you talk about " Nationalisation " people imagine you are going to nationalise everything—even trousers and tooth-brushes—and however great my sympathy might be, I am going to fight any effort to nationalise tooth-brushes for all I am worth. I insist on having my own for my exclusive use. I also insist upon having some chairs and tables and pictures which my father had before me, and to which I am attached for sentimental reasons. Moreover, I don't think it's fair if I choose to live carefully and save a little money that I should not be allowed to enjoy it; and if it makes me unequal to John Jones who blues all his on beer and skittles, well, I say that I am unequal, and am going to remain unequal, and I don't want to abolish the inequality which I believe will always exist. A man has a right to save and to keep his savings. If I were a workman I would want to have my own tools, my saw and my chisel and my hammer. As I am a parson I want to have my own books. I like them, and I can mark them with pencil marks, and scribble absurd comments in the margin, and I want other people to have their books.

'That's where you do harm with your wholesale denunciations. You put the wind up your friends, and you enable the dirty dog who owns the wrong kind of property to advance against you, screened by hosts of decent hard-working people—maiden aunts with only their little annuities to live on, young men with their savings in the post-office, small business people with their little bit of capital on which their livelihood depends, which enables them to carry on independently their perfectly honest work—and because of this screen of women and children the Hun Capitalist can take your trenches every time. What you ought to be out after is not the abolition of all property, but the abolition of the abuse of property. There are certain things which are " property " in the true sense of the word; they naturally and properly belong to a free man, and that we ought to maintain. There are other things which, as Mr. Hobson says, are really " improperty," because they do not properly belong to any individual or any group of individuals, but to the community as a whole. The purpose of property is to secure for a man first the means of serving the community by honest work, and then the reward of his service, and where property does no more than that it ought to be maintained and not abolished. The purpose of " improperty " is to secure to a man first the means of idleness, and then the fruits not of his own but of other people's labours. That ought to be abolished. It is perfectly right that a man's earnings should be his own property with which he can do as he likes legally, though of course morally even these are a trust from God to be used to His honour and glory, and for the welfare of mankind. It is perfectly right that a man's trousers should be his own property, which he can either wear or waste according to his fancy, provided he obeys the laws of decency. It is perfectly right that the copyright of a book which I write, and over which I have laboured, should be my property, and that if I invented a machine the patent right should be my property. On the other hand, it is not right to pay sixteen millions a year in ground rents to so-called property owners in London, and it is not right to pay royalty to coal-owners. It is not right that the profits of combinations and rings, made by keeping up prices, should be the property of the scoundrels who manage to make them. It is of the greatest importance that you should distinguish " property " from " improperty," and the great distinguishing mark between them is that *property is never divorced from service*, it is always the means of doing or the reward for doing honest work; *improperty, on the other hand, is always divorced from service*, and *is the means of securing and preserving idleness*. You only damage your cause when you seek to abolish property along with improperty.'

The Idolatry of Thrift.

Mr. O. L. 'But all that is unpractical nonsense; you cannot make any distinctions, you have got to abolish the whole thing root and branch. Property is always tending to become improperty, and there is a whole lot of it that you cannot be certain about on those lines. You say a man has a right to his savings. Well, has he a right to leave them to his children and his children's children? And has he a right to secure interest on them? Because if you allow that right you get the whole system back again, and under the guise of thrift you start to reward meanness and penalise generosity and open-handedness. You will have people building up big fortunes to secure their children in idleness. And after all, what is the good of saving? It isn't in any way necessary. A man may perform a service to himself if he saves, but he does not perform any service to his fellows.'

Mr. O. C. 'But, pardon me, he does perform a very distinct service. That's where half the trouble lies. You tend to mix up " Capital " and " Capitalists," and to make no distinction between profits and profiteering. If industry is to grow, under whatever system you manage it a certain amount of the total product must be saved to cover the depreciation in value of machinery and tools and unavoidable losses, and to allow for extension, and extension is of vital necessity as long as you have a growing population. Either the community must learn to save or the saving must be done by private individuals, and it is intensely hard at present to get a community to save. Everybody wants it to save, but nobody wants it to save at his expense. They always want the saving to be accomplished at the expense of their next-door neighbour. Here once again you arrive at the necessity for a double motive. Saving is harder than working. For ten men that can work there is only one that can really save. It demands a higher order of intelligence and greater self-control, and is one of the great means of educating people and bringing out those virtues. The man who saves does deserve a reward, does deserve to have his savings secured to him, *and I am sure it would be a loss to abolish all private savings from the world.* But I agree with you that it is necessary that modern communities should learn to save and be their own capitalists, nor do I think that that is impossible. *Only, if it is to be done it means that the motive of service should become stronger and stronger in the community. You will never get efficient public saving in a community which is run on a one-motive basis, and that motive the motive of self-interest.* We come back to the absolute necessity of developing the sadly weakened nobler motive if we are to attain to a rational and moral industrial system. Let us recognise now that the man who saves does perform a service and deserves a reward, because you ought to have no quarrel with " Capital "—that is like quarrelling with your own nose. There is not and there cannot be any quarrel between " Capital " and " Labour," however just a quarrel there may be between " Capitalists " and " Labourers." The accumulation of capital is as great a necessity—and even greater at the present moment—than the production of necessary goods. It is our only hope of so extending our industry and increasing our production as to reach a position where we can produce an adequate living for all—a position

THE DOG COLLAR 115

which we have never yet attained even in our most prosperous days. There is a defence which can be put up on behalf of that much-abused phrase, " the due reward of capital," which really means the due reward of " capitalists," because you cannot reward capital; it's like trying to reward a wash-tub. The capitalist can claim his due reward on these grounds :—

I have performed a service to the State because—
   1. I exercised self-control in saving.
   2. I exercised wit and wisdom in investing.
   3. I exercised courage in risking.

And as long as he really does perform those three services he has a moral right to claim his due reward.'

MR. O. L. ' Yes, but how many of them do ? Most capitalists inherit from their forefathers a comfortable living. They live on the interest of part of it, and pay another man to exercise his wits in taking a minimum risk with the other part of it in order to increase their living by *speculation.* They don't perform any service—or precious little—and I cannot for the life of me see that they have any reward due to them, and certainly they have no right whatever to the enormous rewards which they frequently receive. They have no right to demand twenty and thirty per cent. for practically nothing, and then curse labouring men for trying to get higher wages for hard and distasteful work.'

Mr. O. C. 'I entirely agree with you there, the inheritance of wealth is a very complicated business. We have already recognised by the imposition of death duties that a man has no right to inherit everything that his father decides to leave him; and I firmly believe that those death duties must progressively be increased until inherited wealth tends to disappear somewhere about the third generation, unless each generation performs some service, either of labour or further saving, or both, in order to preserve it. But meanwhile you must recognise that to secure savings on the part of the community as a whole is so vital and important a matter that no statesman can afford to risk the ruin of thrift in his people as individuals, unless he is at the same time training them through moral appeal and education to the difficult task of public saving, and securing a body of public servants at the head of industry and political government who will save as a public duty. When the community has learned the art of public saving and secured men who will put at the service of the community in industry and politics the same wisdom, caution, and courage that is exercised now by capitalists in their own selfish interests, that is, until she can set the accumulation of capital on a two-motive basis, she cannot abolish the capitalist without at the same time saying good-bye to prosperity. It's the same thing all the time—the absolute necessity of the double motive; *as long as we can only rely upon one motive, the present system, or lack of system, with all its faults, is the only one that is practical,* and it is not practical, so there you are: we must either get on to a double-motive basis or bust.

'Of course, there is no doubt that a great deal of this ramp against public servants and their wastefulness is got up, engineered and organised in the Press, by the people who don't want the public services to be efficient, because they want to be able to claim that it is impossible to run industry for the public good rather than for private gain. I am not in the least deceived by that; you can fairly see written in blue pencil all over hundreds of articles that appeal to the daily Press, "Paid for." They are as obviously paid for as the articles in support of the liquor traffic. Business people know that it is to their interest not to miss any opportunity of throwing stones at public bodies, municipal and Government departments. There is no doubt whatever that their inefficiency and wastefulness has been vastly exaggerated, and that a great deal that has been said against them is just pure lying of the lowest and meanest sort. But it remains true that until we have a higher standard of national morality it will be very difficult to secure efficient and disinterested public service. I do not despair of obtaining it, in fact, I am certain that it will be obtained; but neither do I want to shut my eyes to the difficulties and temptations either to reckless extravagance on the one hand, or to equally reckless meanness on the other, that beset and must continue to beset either Government officials or the managers of nationalised industries on whatever system they may be worked. If they depend on votes for their position, they are tempted to follow the crowd and not to lead it, and to become blind leaders of the blind; and if they are made absolute they tend to become as hide-bound and as stupid, and as generally " don't care a damn " as absolute officials have always tended to become.

' There are endless difficulties and infinite dangers besetting the higher order in industry and in politics, *but they are all moral and spiritual difficulties and dangers.* Given a higher order of public morality and private virtue, all sorts of economic possibilities in reform open out before us; without that we have got to go on as we are very largely, or grow steadily worse. You can only work a better system with better people, and that is why I appeal to you again—appeal with all the earnestness that I possess, by the passion of Labour and its age-long suffering, by the agony of Europe and by its bloody sweat, and if I believed it would have force with you as it has with me, I would add by the travail pains of God and His great love for us. I would appeal to you not to hold aloof from us in our great organised effort to create the better people, who shall be able to create and preserve in being the better order.'

Profit-mongers and wage slaves cannot be good men.

Mr. O. L. 'We would not hold aloof from you if we believed that your organised effort was going to do any good, but we don't. It seems to us to be a mug's game. How are you going to get this moral appeal home to people?

Do you think it's going to be done by sermons and services and lectures? Is that the way you are going to make the better people who shall be able to create and preserve in being the better order? I cannot think how you can be such fat-heads as to suppose that it is possible. It is in the workshop, in the factory, and in the office that men's characters are formed. Even when you get them to church—which is not very often you'll admit—it's only for an hour or so, and they listen there to your moral appeal for unselfishness and the dignity of labour, and then go out to work anything from forty-eight to sixty hours a week under a system which has not an ounce of unselfishness or an ounce of moral decency in it.

'It's just the same with the capitalist. He may be a church-warden on Sundays, but he is a profit-seeker on Mondays, and it's his profit-seeking not his churchwardening that forms and moulds his character.

'It is ridiculous to suppose that you are going to make better people by setting them to sing hymns, and say prayers, and listen to sermons. Once they get out in the world all your moral appeal flows off them like water off a duck's back. It goes in at one ear and out at another. They have to come out of their moral dreams back to their immoral reality, and it is the immoral reality that forms the character. You are never going to make better people out of profiteers and wage slaves. As long as people produce for profit and not for use, and work for a wage and not for service, you can never make them anything but purely selfish people.'

Mr. O. C. 'That really means that you go back, as indeed you are always going back, to the essential falsehood that rots your whole position and paralyses your whole movement from a moral point of view. You will insist that systems make men, and that men do not make systems, whereas indeed neither of those statements is true, and the inquiry as to which of them is the truth is like the inquiry with regard to a dog running down a street with a tin can tied to its tail, as to whether the tin rattles because the dog runs or the dog runs because the tin rattles.

'Men are not entirely the product of the system of profit-seeking and wage slavery, as you call it ; there is in them a moral nature which has not been killed, and cannot be killed. Moreover, you overrate the necessary moral degradation in the present system. There are a large number of business men who are not profit-seekers in any bad sense, for, mind you, it is a ridiculous economic fallacy to suppose that under any system industry would not have to make it one of its objects to secure a profit on the year's workings. It is certainly an inevitable law—a really inevitable law independent of psychology—that you cannot get out of a pint pot more than you put into it. Even if you regard the nation as an industrial unit and permit the running of a certain number of industries which are not profitable, and either only just pay their way or do not pay their way, those industries must then live and extend upon the larger profits made out of the paying industries. It might be justifiable to run railways at a loss, but it would only be justifiable provided you ran other things at a greater gain.

' It is absolutely essential that we get clear in our minds that the accumulation of capital wealth, whoever holds it and whoever manages it, is a vital necessity. Mr. Keynes puts his finger on the pulse of that question when he says that the one real benefit of the nineteenth-century industrialism was its immense accumulation of capital, which to the great benefit of mankind was built up during the half century before the war, and that these accumulations were possible for two reasons : first because " the labouring classes accepted through ignorance or powerlessness, or were compelled, persuaded, or cajoled by custom, convention, authority, and the well-established order of society, into accepting a situation in which they could call their own very little of the cake that they and nature and the capitalist were co-operating to produce; and on the other hand the capitalist classes were allowed to call the best part of the cake theirs, and were theoretically free to consume it, on the tacit underlying condition that they consumed very little of it in practice. The duty of saving became nine-tenths of virtue, and the growth of the cake (*i.e.* capital wealth) the object of true religion."

'Now these two reasons have very largely ceased to exist. The labouring classes can no longer be deceived or driven into accepting starvation wages, and the capitalist classes have largely started to spend instead of saving; and these two things have happened at a time when we have wasted and destroyed a large amount of capital wealth—that capital wealth which is an absolute necessity for the preservation and extension of industry, and therefore an absolute necessity for maintaining the standard of life of the people. That means that industry as a whole must be, and (if our population grows as it is almost bound to do, given anything like settlement and peace) must continue to be, a profit-seeking concern.

'In its endeavour to make an industry pay, that is, provide a sufficiency for all concerned in it, and a surplus product to add to the total capital wealth, the industrial captain is pursuing a perfectly moral and legitimate end, and I maintain there are a good number of captains of industry who are working for that perfectly legitimate and moral end now. The phrase " production for use and not for profit " requires a good deal of examining. Profit is not such an entirely disreputable thing as is often made out. It is not the production for profit that is in itself wrong, but the production for *personal profit* from selfish motives, and the determination to put that purpose first and foremost, and to disregard all other considerations, *and that is a moral and spiritual matter again.* Even now there are good captains of industry and bad captains of industry, and it is fatal to lump them both into a class and regard them as incapable of listening to a moral appeal. And if the phrase " production for use and not for profit" requires examination, so does all this cant about wage slavery.

'That a man should work for a wage is not of necessity or in itself degrading; it depends very much upon how he looks at it. He may make that his sole and only object, in which case it is degrading. He may regard it as a side issue—a very important side issue, and one which he has to give attention to, but nevertheless a side issue—his main object being to uphold the dignity of his craft by good work and the maintaining of an honourable tradition. There is no essential difference between wages and salaries. A salary is only a day wage paid by the quarter, and there are thousands of salaried workers who regard their salaries not indeed as being unimportant, but certainly not as being all-important, and who are perfectly unconscious of any degradation in receiving them. And there is no inherent reason why wage-earners should not do the same, and there are, as a matter of fact, a good many wage-earners who look at things in that way. I do not regard the present system as being so inherently evil and so utterly untinged with anything noble that it has been able to kill the moral power of my fellow-citizens, and make them finally impervious to moral appeal.'

Mr. O. L. 'Good Lord, you are an innocent, aren't you? No difference between wages and salary? Of course there is. The wage-earner is never sure, he can be dismissed at a week's notice, he doesn't know when he is going to find himself on the streets with nothing a week, and he's got no part to play in the management of his industry. A change in machinery and the introduction of a new productive process may throw him on the streets with nothing. The community may gain, but he stands to lose, and has stood to lose all through the centuries. There's no encouragement for him to work for any object but his wage. Why should he care about the business as a whole? As a matter of fact he doesn't, and he works for Friday night and for Friday night alone. He knows that the industry cares nothing for him, and regards him as a hand and nothing else. Then why on earth should he care for it?'

Mr. O. C. 'Well, if I'm innocent you are muddle-headed. Everything you say is true, but none of it need necessarily continue to be true because a man works for wages. Insurance systems could be started to secure the worker against want. They would not of course secure him against unemployment. The cure of that is a deep and difficult problem. But he could be given reasonable security against want. Measures to bring that about could be pressed for and carried through, and would command a very large measure of support from decent people of all classes, including captains of industry. And in that matter once again religion has a part to play. One of the great practical difficulties in the working of unemployment insurance measures is dishonesty among the workers. It is necessary to take elaborate and expensive precautions against fraud. A complicated system of inquiries has to be kept up, because men and women will take advantage of the authorities and claim money when they do not need it. Their social sense is not strong enough to make them feel the disgrace and degradation of a fraud upon the community. You know that is true; the community cannot do its duty by the worker unless the worker becomes more keenly conscious of his duty to the community. Here again co-operation between us would be of enormous benefit to us both. All sorts of plans could be carried out if we could absolutely rely upon the morals of the workers. The present schemes work extravagantly, and harshly, because we cannot rely upon it.

'It is true, of course, that the growth of limited liability companies and combines has tended to destroy the human relationship between employers and employed. But that I believe is not beyond remedy while the man still remains a wage-earner. That again is very much a matter of morale on both sides, and the spread of the welfare movement goes to show that many captains of industry are realising their responsibility.'

Mr. O. L. 'Oh yes, they are realising it now because they see that it is profitable for them, they are giving the workers sops to keep them quiet, and secure the industrial peace which is necessary for their profits. They have found out that it pays them, and that's why they do it. I tell you it's profit, profit, profit, that's all they care about, and that's the only object they have.'

Mr. O. C. 'Red spectacles again. What the devil right have you to assume all that? I say you are plum-bung wrong, and that the motives of welfare work are like all other human motives —good and bad. Many a captain of industry backs up welfare work, not only because it pays, but because he likes to see his workpeople happy and contented, and hates to think of their working under bad conditions. I say that you do any amount of damage by this imputing of bad motives to movements that are good in themselves, and this insistence that all employers are purely selfish. I think they are just about as selfish as your people, not much more and not much less. What you ought to do is to encourage and back up the good employer and down the scoundrel, just as you ought to encourage and back up the good workman and down the slacker. Even now it ought to be possible to make your Unions not merely unions of men to secure more wages, but unions of men to do more honest and better work, and more of it, unions for the promotion of *esprit de corps* and pride in your work.'

Luxury pleads poverty with its tongue in its cheek.

Mr. O. L. ' We cannot get it because the workers are constantly irritated by the utter injustice of the whole system. We see Labour prostituted on all hands to base and loathsome purposes. Just think of what the feelings of a workman are when he takes up the *Daily Mirror*, and sees the pictures of the women's dresses at Ascot, and reads descriptions of champagne lunches and society divorces, and then thinks of the slums of Sheffield and of his comrades in the blast furnaces destroying their health and ruining their capacity for enjoyment, to produce what? To produce wealth, which is used up in this swinish exhibition of sensuality. What's the good of talking to him about the accumulation of capital and the necessity of saving with that sort of business going on? The accumulation of capital is absolutely essential you say for the production of necessaries, because we are so poor, and you expect the worker to believe it with Ascot and the Regent Street shops and all the endless array of rotten luxuries flaunted continually before his eyes. Is it likely that he is going to stint and starve himself, and be content with what people magnanimously say he ought to have—a living wage, for hard and strenuous labour—when these swine get away with enormous incomes to waste and squander? And what's it all caused by? Why, the bad distribution of the wealth there is. It's a problem of distribution I tell you. These huge incomes are a curse, because they not only waste the money which you admit we very badly need as capital to extend useful and productive industries, but they divert an enormous amount of our productive power to luxury which is no use either to those who consume it or to those who produce it. I contend that it is thoroughly bad for a man to have an income of £10,000 a year, and thoroughly bad for the community of which he is a member; it enables him to buy things he ought not to buy, to employ labour for purposes for which it ought not to be employed, and to live in a style in which it is not right that any man should live.'

MR. O. C. 'I agree with you all the road—all the road right up to the end. Ascot makes you sick at a time like this, or indeed at any time—swinish, that's the only word for it—and I agree that there is a problem of distribution. It is true, of course, that the redistribution of all the incomes over £500 a year would not solve the problem of poverty. You have to allow for legitimate expenditure on State services which are not productive, on charitable and humane objects, universities, homes for the blind, crippled, feeble-minded, etc., all of which are now supported by the wealth of the wealthy, and would have to be supported somehow. Though, of course, the need for some such expenses would disappear with the coming of better social conditions, yet a good many would continue necessary under any conditions. Allowing for this, redistribution would not solve our problem—we should still be poor, we should not have enough. But that makes it all the more necessary that no part of our income should be wasted. If, as is true, we cannot now afford necessaries for all, still less can we afford idiotic luxury for some. If we cannot pay the workers properly, still less can we afford to pay idlers exorbitantly.

'But is that sort of expenditure and that way of living a necessity of the present system, or is it an abuse of it? Need the private capitalist of necessity be a pig? Might he not be made into a man? Once again, is there not here a necessity for the two motives and the moral appeal? Surely what we have got to do is to create a public opinion which condemns and despises this way of living, which condemns and despises idleness and sensuality; and is there really any other way of meeting the difficulty? Do you really think that you can by mere reorganisation of the system make men out of swine? Sumptuary laws have not in the past been very successful. As long as people desire these things, as long as they demand them, they will be supplied. Isn't the only way to deal with it—as long as you are going to leave men free—to create by moral appeal and example a fashion of public opinion which makes luxurious living disreputable, and by decreasing the demand puts a stop to the supply? Does not demand create supply in these as in other matters?'

Mr. O. L. 'No, it's a question of abnormal purchasing power. These men and women indulge in this swinish exhibition because they still have abnormal purchasing power, even though they pay enormous sums in taxation. A man and his wife of whom I have heard have an income of £150,000 a year. They pay £87,000 in taxation, but that leaves them with a purchasing power of £63,000 a year, which is rotten bad for them and for the community; and if you dared to tax them any further, like as not they would clear out and live anywhere else on the earth. Yet I maintain that somehow or other that abnormal purchasing power must not be allowed to continue in the hands of individuals—it puts too much of a strain on human nature.'

Mr. O. C. 'I entirely agree, and I am sure that the super-tax ought to be run up to the utmost limit; but unless you combine with that an appeal to the moral sense of the community I see no real way out of luxury expenditure. You must not only endeavour to check the supply which you say creates demand, but you must endeavour to deal with the demand itself, because it arises out of a very deep-seated passion in human nature. Luxury expenditure is not confined to one class, it is found in all classes, and among all men. It has its root in sensuality, and sensuality in man is insatiable, and can only be limited in two ways, one by suppressing it and forcibly taking away the power of indulging it, which is largely what you suggest, and the other and better way, by providing a higher and more distinctly human outlet for it.

'You see, the reason for luxury expenditure is the same in all classes. In common human language you can say it is the desire of joy. All men and women want joy, that is, they want something more to live for than the humdrum, they want something that bites and burns and takes them out of themselves—they are looking for something red. The most prosaic and humdrum person in the world is consciously or unconsciously the pilgrim of romance, adventure, excitement. From that root desire comes the love of drinking, gambling, the sensuous art of undressing which is the modern form of dress, and the passion for pleasure which is the distinctive feature of our times. They are all the result of the natural, human craving for joy, and as long as men seek to satisfy that craving with purely material things, it grows stronger as they feed it. Even as we are now, the ordinary working man of England would rather that you interfere with anything almost than his beer. Beer stands to him for joy, and the drink bill of the current year is estimated to amount to almost £500,000,000, or £11 per head of the population of the United Kingdom, and when we remember that this average gives £11 to all women, children, and teetotallers, some idea of the amount spent on intoxicants by the drinking part of the population can be imagined.

'Everywhere this desire of sensual joy appears to be growing stronger, and I want you to grasp that it is insatiable, that the more you feed it the stronger it grows, and that it tends to make men more and more selfish. A great deal of the force behind your movement is the force of this desire. Men see in it increased wages and greater opportunities for sensual indulgence of all sorts, and they come to your movement with *sensuality and selfishness as their driving motive*, although, of course, with the usual human genius for self-deception, they clothe it in the garments of altruism, and deck it with the diamonds of higher morality. Now nothing is more certain than that the co-operative commonwealth which you and I seek cannot be made out of selfish and sensual people; it will demand of necessity unselfishness and self-control, and that is your great difficulty: you seek to prepare the workers of the world for the tremendous task of carrying on the co-operative commonwealth by making to them what is very largely a selfish appeal.'

The Unselfishness of Labour.

Mr. O. L. 'Oh yes, we have heard all that before. I'm not denying that two of the greatest enemies of the working people are drink and sensuality—no one who knows the facts could deny it—but I do deny that our appeal is primarily a selfish one. We constantly find in addressing the workers that it is the appeal to self-sacrifice and co-operation that has real force with them; and I believe that education, combined with a reformed system of industry, will do away with this danger altogether.'

Mr. O. C. 'I wish I could believe you were right, but I doubt it. I doubt if you estimate rightly the human capacity for self-deception, and the enormous power of the human passion for romance, excitement, and adventure. I think one reason why you underestimate is that your Labour leaders find satisfaction for your passion and craving for excitement in this very fight; it is very largely your life, and it is that life which you seek to give them. But the fight cannot provide a permanent basis for living, and if that is the only substitute you have to give for sensuality, it is pitifully inadequate. As to education, it depends upon what sort of education it is. If it is the education which merely enlarges men's minds and quickens their imaginations and increases their knowledge, it is more likely to intensify than satisfy the hunger for romance, for that which stings and burns. These very people that make swine of themselves at Ascot belong to what are called the educated classes, who have the world of the mind opened to them to explore; but it does not appear to satisfy them. And now I come to my great point. I am pretty sure from my knowledge of human nature, both from personal study of it and from the findings of the psychologists, that the great natural human outlet for this passion for joy is the outlet of religion. It is by the aid of religion that duty can be turned into joy; it is when the world becomes God's world that people's souls can be satisfied with simple things. Without God men crave for an ever-increasing complexity of sensual excitement; with God they can rest in the peace that passeth understanding, which is the most exciting thing in the world. It is this psychological truth that lies behind the famous Marxian statement that " religion is opium to the people." It is opium because it provides a reasonable and satisfying outlet for those passions which, unless they find it, keep them in a constant state of surging discontent, and make them good revolutionaries but bad citizens, good fighters but incapable of co-operation for any large and unselfish purpose.

'And here again we come to the vital necessity of religion to your movement; without it I believe it can only issue in anarchy, disruption, and decay. The greatest danger to the co-operative commonwealth is this cloud of sensuality and materialism that has settled down not merely upon the spendthrifts but upon the workers of the world; and I know of no other light that can pierce that cloud and disclose the better world beyond, the world of simple joys and homely duties, of kindly affection and self-sacrifice, in sight of which stable states and happy homes can be built, I know of no other light but that which shines in the face of Jesus of Nazareth. The craving for romance which leads to luxury expenditure is nothing but the perverted cry of men's souls for God.'

The Churches funk the Brewers.

Mr. O. L. 'Well, there may be something in that. I am willing to confess that there are a good number of Labour leaders who are troubled in their minds about these questions of drink and materialism and sensuality. You will remember in his book on *Labour and the New World* Mr. Philip Snowden says that " if the working classes would spend one-twentieth part of the money that they now waste in drink and gambling on political and publicity organisation, the Capitalist monopoly of the means of influencing public opinion would be quickly destroyed."

'But there you come to the system again; behind the drink traffic there is this cursed vested interest. Our present system of managing the drink traffic is a public disgrace. Although it is true, as Mr. Justice Salter stated at the Leeds

Assizes in December 1920, that " half the crime of the country is caused by drink, and it is indirectly responsible for a good part of the other half," still we persist in allowing the exploitation of the people by the drink traffic, for profit. That's what makes my blood boil. In this matter perhaps more than in any other you see how supply creates demand. The workers have drink hurled at their heads, traps are laid to catch them at their very doors, and it's one of the best paying concerns even now. It simply means that in the name of freedom this blighted brewing interest is allowed to degrade and debauch the people's mind, and here, if anywhere, there is need of drastic and radical reform, and that's one of my grouses against your Church. You have never taken this question up in earnest, you have confined yourselves very largely to personal moral appeals to the workers to resist the temptation to drink, but because many of you have shares in breweries, and because you are afraid of attacking vested interests, you have not dared to go for the traffic and urge the necessity of taking it out of private hands, and thus dissolving this hateful league between two of the lowest passions in human nature—intemperance and greed of gold. Nor have you properly considered how enormously drink is due to bad housing, poverty, and evil conditions of work. The Nonconformist churches have been much better in this respect than you have, and I am willing to admit that the workers owe them a debt of gratitude for the work that they have done in the temperance cause; but I am sure that we can never get rid of the drink evil until we get rid of the brewing interests and the caucus of the liquor traffic who are continually influencing parliamentary legislation to bolster up the source of their dividends.'

Mr. O. C. 'I am with you all the way, and I believe an increasing number of churchmen are with you too, and this is a matter in which more cordial relations between our two movements would tend to strengthen the hands of both. If we could really join hands and form a partnership in this matter, determined to create a sober Britain, I believe we could do it, but although I entirely agree with you that there can be no efficient dealing with this question which does not include an attack upon drink as a vested interest, and although I agree too that the Church in the past has been slack in these matters and has not as a body recognised how much the drinking habits of the workers were caused by their conditions, still I believe that in order to cure the drinking habit you must go to the root of the matter in the soul of the individual man. If you are going to cure him of drink and sensuality you must provide him with the proper human substitute for it, and I am convinced that the proper human substitute for spirits is the Spirit, and that men will always tend to fill themselves with new-made wine unless their life is touched here and there and transformed by the love of God. And moreover, although I have the greatest contempt for the cant that is talked about non-interference with individual freedom, which would make it a cloak for any sort of licence, yet I am sure that in thinking of this question we touch upon the very roots of a deeper and a wider one. The man who said that he would rather see England free than England sober used an epigram which is as true and as false as most epigrams. We would agree about its falsehood, but I am not sure that we would agree about the measure of its truth. The great problem of all human society is the combination of personal freedom and social order, and the constant danger is that we over-emphasise one at the expense of the other. Granted that the nineteenth-century statesmen and politicians greatly exaggerated the value of freedom, and that their idolatry of it produced a world which meant, and still means, practical slavery for a large number of people, that ought to warn deep-thinking men against a swing of the pendulum which would lead us to underrate the value of what they so vastly overrated, and land us out of the frying-pan of *laissez-faire* into the fire of bureaucratic tyranny. It is the fear of that fire of tyranny and interference with personal liberty that is the main drawback in the eyes of most ordinary men and women to your political programme. In all sorts of ways you propose to fix and determine people's duties for them, leaving them but very little choice, and large numbers of people doubt if you really understand how far you would have to go if you once started upon that course of action. Although all decent people desire that some sort of order should issue out of the present chaos, they are gravely in doubt as to whether the effort to force that order would not finally lead to chaos worse confounded, because it would mean the attempt to suppress irrepressible human instincts. Granted that the largest industry in Britain is, as Sir L. G. Chiozza-Money says, " the manufacture of rubbish which is neither use nor ornament," it is a fact that the manufacture prospers because there is a demand for rubbish — people want it. It may be wrong of them to want it, but they do. They want cheap jewellery and hideous furniture and ridiculous clothes, and cheap and vulgar luxuries, and because they demand them they are supplied. Your way of dealing with that is to say that they ought not to want them, and that therefore you are not going to let them have them, and you are going forcibly to prevent the supply of them. The great question is as to whether that is good for the people, and whether you ought not rather to set about the tremendous task of changing public taste. The same difficulty lies behind phrases like " the right to work." If you grant that a man has the right to work, are you going to grant that he has a right to work in whatever place and at whatever job he likes? and has he the right if he does not like a job to change it and go to another one? and supposing he likes an odd job like selling children's gollywogs in the Strand or grinding people's knives at their own doors, must the State find him a job of that kind?

'Of course those are extreme cases,

THE DOG COLLAR 157

but they are only types. If you grant that a man has a right to choose his place of work and his job and to change it when he likes, then the task of finding regular employment for him or of feeding him when he is out of employment becomes enormously difficult. If, on the other hand, you are prepared to sacrifice freedom for order, and the authorities are allowed to dictate as to where and at what a man shall work, it becomes considerably easier—but dangerous.

'My own feeling is that you have got to go canny with the limitations you put upon people's personal freedom, or you may find yourself sitting on the top of a volcano which does not know from moment to moment whether it is going to erupt or not. Here again we plainly see the absolute necessity for a change of heart and mind in the people before we can hope to work industries on a co-operative system. You will perhaps remember the passage in Karl Kautsky's *Terrorism and Communism*, in which he says:—

' " If it is desired to abolish capitalism some form of organisation must be created which will be able to function as well, if not better, without the capitalist head. This demands a proletariate which is conscious of its duties not only towards its own neighbour and comrades, but also towards society as a whole—a proletariate, moreover, which has become accustomed *to voluntary discipline.*"

' Now that is a phrase which I think you and your party ought all to lay well to heart, " a proletariate which has become accustomed to voluntary discipline." Without that voluntary discipline I see no final solution of our problems and no possibility of attaining to order. In the final issue the order which we obtain must be largely voluntary. That, of course, means education, and unfortunately education takes time, but in addition to education I am convinced that it also means religion. The voluntary discipline of men's passions, lusts, and anti-social desires needs more than new knowledge, it needs new power.

'Let me explain by taking a definite instance. There is a very common error abroad to-day that the mere giving of information upon the facts of sex to young people will enable them to resist temptation and keep their bodies clean. I do not know anything which is further from the truth; mere knowledge has no power to subdue passion. Thousands of men who know perfectly well the personal risks they run, and the public sin which they commit, will indulge in promiscuous fornication; and it is precisely the same with the love of luxury, ease, idleness, and sensual pleasure. In order that men may voluntarily discipline themselves in regard to these things it is necessary that they have something which in a measure takes their place, something which gives to them the joy and the interest which they afford. In other words, the only thing which is strong enough to meet a passion is a counter-passion, and it is that counter-passion for God revealed in man that Christ can give, and it is on those grounds that I say that religion, or the passion for God in man, is a necessity if the proletariate are to be fitted for the nationalised and internationalised system of life.

'Behind all these schemes and plans for organising the better world and the national and international commonwealth there lies the necessity either of reforming human nature or of forcing it into a certain form. There are many who declare that human nature cannot be reformed, but for my part I am certain that it cannot be forced into any form. There is that in human nature which in the long run will break any tyranny from outside that is imposed upon it. Discipline to be lasting must come from within, and no dream of the idealist is half so Utopian and impracticable as this dream which haunts and has always haunted men's minds, of forcing mankind into a certain preconceived and symmetrical plan. If we want to do any really fruitful work for the world as a whole, we simply must recognise that although the human race may be an organism it is not, and can never be made into a mechanism. It may grow into something harmonious and beautiful, and we can foster and help that growth, but it can never be forced into it.

'The conflict between the organic and the mechanical conception of human society is one of the most real issues in the world, and to my mind there is only one side to take, and that is the side of the organism.

'We are really back again here upon the question of force, and we come to the same great truth, that force is never creative; at best, and very doubtfully, it is only preventive of disaster.'

So called Religious Education worse than useless.

Mr. O. L. 'Well, on the whole I am inclined to agree with you on that question, and to be quite candid it is on that very issue that the Labour Movement bids fair to split. That is where sane Labour differs from the Reds. It is the crux of direct action, because deep within us we feel that the better world which we desire cannot be brought about in that way. There is, I suppose you know, only a very small section of the British Labour Movement which would interpret Marx as Lenin and Trotsky do; most of us, if we follow him at all, interpret him rather according to Kautsky, and believe above all other things in the necessity of an educated democracy. Our great problem is the problem of securing that. We are doing our best through our Labour Colleges, through the Workers' Educational Association, and by the encouragement in working men's clubs of classes and lectures. We have very little faith in the education which is provided for our children by the State. It is designed mainly to fit them to take their part in the competitive struggle for existence which the Capitalist system of industry makes necessary. It does not really educate the children socially or politically, it makes them individuals whose lives are governed by the one idea of getting on. We do not trust much in what is called education now, and, to be quite frank, we fail entirely to see what good religion does and what purpose it serves. The objects of religious education seem to be to produce mild, narrow-minded, and submissive people with little or no social sense, who would never have the self-sacrifice or the initiative to protest against any wrong which did not affect them personally. They are taught to be humble, meek, mild, and forgiving, and the result is that deadly selfish apathy about social matters which is the greatest obstacle to our work.

'As far as religion is concerned as a factor in education, it seems to us to be a hindrance rather than a help. As a child I was taught to believe that God made the world in six days, that it would all have been a perfectly good show if Eve hadn't eaten an apple, but after that it was cursed; that God chose out the people of the Jews and set them to fight their way in a series of bloody and barbarous battles into the promised land; that He told their leaders to behave like the vilest Prussian Junkers, and kill men, women, and children without mercy. I was told that these wars were God's will, and that He Himself was the God of battles and the Author of plagues, diseases, and famine, which He sent upon men as a judgment for their sins. And then I was told that in order to give men a chance because He loved the world He sent His beloved Son Jesus Christ to suffer the agony on the Cross which we deserved, and that if we accepted Him as our Saviour we would be saved from hell, but that all the people who did not accept Him and all the heathens who never heard of Him were to be damned eternally.

'That is what I was taught, and as far as I know it is what the workers' children are being taught still, and you will excuse me being emphatic, but I'm damned if I see what use it all is; most of it's false, and a great deal of it's positively evil. At the best it fills the children's minds up with a lot of lumber, and at the worst it sends them out into the world believing in a lot of lies and still totally ignorant upon all matters that affect their social conduct.'

Mr. O. C. 'There is an awful lot of that with which I am in entire agreement. A great deal of what we were taught as children, and of what children are still being taught in the name of religion, does seem to me to be not only useless but thoroughly bad. But I would ask you this, have you given a true impression of what your religious education meant to you, bad as it was? Was it not dominated and controlled almost entirely by one figure, the figure of Jesus of Nazareth? From your very earliest days were you not taught to associate goodness with Jesus? Looking back, can you remember a time when you did not think that being good meant being like Him? Were you not always taught too that to be religious meant following in His steps? Did you not have the picture of the Saviour with the children on His knees or the lamb in His arms, or the Saviour surrounded by the sick and suffering, calling the weary and heavy-laden to Him, fiercely rebuking the proud and the hypocritical, tenderly receiving the publican and the sinner, caring for His mother in His agony on the Cross, forgiving the thief who railed upon Him, dying a gallant death and rising again to lead men on into the paths of brotherhood and peace ? Were you not taught that to follow in His steps, to be loving as He was loving, to stand up for right as He stood up for it, to be pure as He was pure, was to attain the highest kind of manhood, and were you not taught to seek Him in prayer ?

'Friend, I was taught all the lies that you were taught, and through it all I still was taught one truth, that He was IT, absolutely IT, and that is the truth that has stuck. The lies I have shed, fought my way out of, the truth remains and is the best thing I have in my life. Now look back honestly, and tell me if that was not partly so with you.

'I found among British soldiers in the field, even those who had long since severed their connection with any organised Christian Church, a gentleness and courtesy, a consideration for the rights of others, a reasonableness and love of fair play, and I found too an almost universal respect for the Carpenter of Nazareth. Don't you think that I am justified in connecting those two things, especially as I find them so very closely connected in the experience of my own life and in my own soul? It is that treasure which I feel it would have been a disaster for me to be without, it is that treasure which I feel it would be a disaster if our children were to go without. It is to that quiet, silent, but persistent power of the living Jesus that

I look mainly as the redemptive power which is needed in the world. Without that idea, without that living person, to be quite honest, I have very little hope indeed.'

Mr. O. L. 'Well, that's the other side of it, and I'm going to confess that although I do not feel as strongly as you do about it, it has had a certain power in my life too, but what I am not clear about is that it all could not have been done better in another way. Supposing I had been taught no lies but only the truth, supposing there had been put before me in a really attractive form the history of the social struggle of our race, supposing I had been told the truth of our gradual evolution from the beast, and how through suffering and sorrow, led by the army of martyrs, men had marched down a bloody and yet glorious road that led them out of darkness into light, and that of all the martyrs Jesus of Nazareth was perhaps the greatest, that His crucifixion stood in a long line of other calvaries, and only differed from them in degree and not in kind. Supposing I had been taught to love humanity rather than God, and the history of humanity had been given to me in such a way as to catch my imagination and inspire my devotion, would I not have been better off, better off because I would have had less lumber to carry and no dark mist of lies to dim the truth of the brotherhood of man which is the only truth ? '

Mr. O. C. ' I think you would have been better off—in fact, I think you would almost have received the ideal religious education for a child as far as the teaching of truth is concerned, but I still think that it would have left something vital out. I said that I found among men in France gentleness, courtesy, and consideration for the rights of others, and that I connected that with the almost universal respect for Jesus of Nazareth, but if I am to be honest I must also add that I found among men in France the lowest and most bestial kind of sensuality, callousness, cruelty, and the crudest kind of selfishness. I found in them not merely ignorance of their duties to their fellows, but a certain amount of wilful defiance of the duties that they saw. To sum it up, I found among them quite definite and distinct sin, and I am persuaded that their greatest need and the world's greatest need is redemption from that sin. I believe that you underrate its power in the life of man, and that you are blind to the extent to which it makes perfectly impossible schemes and plans for the better organisation of our social life. I believe that you are far too prone to regard men as the naturally virtuous victims of a vicious system imposed upon them from without, rather than as the vicious and wilfully sinful creators of a system which has grown up from within. I believe that you are blind to what is the essential fact, that what you call the Capitalist System is an outward growth which very closely corresponds to the inward nature of mankind as it is.

'The events of the last five years ought surely to have made us wiser if sadder men. They ought surely to have warned us that there is within every one of us, within the very best of us, a beast—a dirty, selfish, crude, and cruel beast. We ought in the light of the fierce glare of truth which has been beating upon human souls during these years to have seen deep enough to perceive that man needs not only education but redemption—needs not only teaching which will show him what his duty is, but power to overcome the beast within him and perform that high and noble duty when he sees it. It is that power which I believe Jesus has for men, but He has it only when He takes for them the value not merely of the greatest of all dead teachers, but the value of the greatest of living leaders, or in a word the value of God. In Jesus as God I believe lies the hope of the world and its only hope —in Jesus as God I believe lies the hope of your movement and its only hope.'

The weakness of the Church has destroyed the power of the Christ.

Mr. O. L. ' When you talk like that I can't help feeling that there is something in it, and yet obviously, if you are sincere, you have a feeling for Jesus of Nazareth which I cannot share. I cannot altogether separate Him as you seem to do from the multitude of falsehoods that have been taught in His name, or from all that ruck of obsolete theories as the centre of which He was first presented to me. Nor can I reconcile Him altogether with His representatives here on earth, and that is what I must do if I am, as a representative of Organised Labour, to promote relations with Organised Christianity. I frankly confess that the happenings of the past few years have made me feel differently about human nature, they have made me feel that we need something to lift us up on to a higher level, and I do perceive that if we could really practise what Christ taught, if we could really run our politics on the basis of the Sermon on the Mount, the better world would come and come quickly. I am going to be quite frank with you, as I believe you have been with me, and tell you that there have been times when I sat alone, and thought about these things and about my own life, that I have longed for some power that would make me a better man in order that I might make this people a better people. Of course one does not say those things except to pals, and I have been accustomed to regard it rather as a mood than as anything of real importance, but from what I can see it is something more than a mood with you.

'If I could see in your churches any real sign of that power, if I could be persuaded that it was to be got through your services and religious exercises, I think you would almost have persuaded me that an alliance between us would make for the best welfare of the labouring people. But you know I don't perceive any sign of it—I find in your churches and in your clergymen a spirit of narrow-minded bickering, prejudice, and hatred. You tell me that you sometimes feel bitterly angry when you read the Labour papers; well, I often feel angry and contemptuous when I read the Church papers, and especially the letters from correspondents. Do you honestly believe that the mentality which they display is in the least likely to lead to a more united world and a higher level of living?'

Mr. O. C. 'No I don't. The Religious and the Labour papers appear to me to be among the worst papers in the world. But just as I have vision enough to perceive that the Labour Press does not represent the soul of your movement, and would not allow its bitterness, narrowness, and rancour to stand in the way of active co-operation between Christ's Church and the workers of the world, so I would plead with you to have the vision to see that the Religious Press does not represent the soul of the Church, and not to allow its bitterness and party spirit to stand in the way of friendship and co-operation between us.

'Both our organised bodies are failures,

as organised bodies are bound to be. Both have their blots and blemishes, both come tumbling down from the sublime to the ridiculous, yet about both there is something sublime, and it is on the level of the sublime, high enough to be charitable to the ridiculous, that I think we ought to meet. At any rate, what it means, if our dreams are to come true, is a world-wide moral and religious revival. Without that I see no prospect of better days ahead, do you? And I do not see any other instrument with which it can be brought about than that which is provided by the churches of Christ in this and other lands.'

The Unions are better brotherhoods than the Churches.

Mr. O. L. ' Wouldn't it be far better to bring it about through the people's organisations? Wouldn't it be far better to work through the Unions and the International Workers' Fellowship throughout the world ? Wouldn't it be better to separate the idea of Jesus from the name—the name which has become so degraded and defiled by the misuse that has been made of it ? I cannot see how Jesus can be delivered from the religious bigotry, blindness, and intolerance with which He is associated in millions of the workers' minds. It seems to me to be far more hopeful to work for a moral revival through the brotherhood of the Workers' Unions than to attempt to produce it through the chaos of the Christian churches. Honestly, it seems to me that our unions are better brotherhoods than your churches.'

Mr. O. C. ' I wonder. I have often thought of that. I have often wished, terrible as it sounds, that Jesus could find a new name, a name which we had not sullied, dirtied, and defiled by our infidelity, our blindness, and our sin. But when I think again I feel that that is wrong. Surely the fact that His name still lives and still calls—calls with a tremendous power, as it does to some of us even now—is in itself almost a miracle. As a writer in the *Free Thinker* remarked not long ago, " The miracle of the physical resurrection of Jesus Christ pales into insignificance before the miracle of the persistence and continual revival of the religion that He founded."

' Although the writer regarded it as honeycombed with superstition, uncertain in its origin, and discredited by its failure, he was unable to blind himself to the miracle of its continuous revival. It is the resurrection after the crucifixion over and over again, and it is in this name, " crucified but unconquerable," that I believe the power of man's redemption lies. If you will forgive me putting it as it appears to me, it is because Jesus calls us with hands still wounded and feet still pierced, and with the crown of thorns still sideways on His head, with the kiss of traitor friends still wet upon His lips and the spittle of the world's wild mockery still streaming down His face—it is that which adds to His intensely human pleading a power and a fire that I can only call divine.

'And so when I finish my thinking I come to the conclusion that I want no new name, I am content, and believe that the world at last will come to be well content with the old one that is ever new.

'And then with regard to your unions being better brotherhoods than our churches. I wonder. Supposing you were to start a new Union and were to go out seeking members, and when they came and asked you what they were going to get out of it you were to reply, " Nothing, not a ha'penny. This is a Union not to get but to give. You not only will not get any benefits of a material sort, but you will be asked to give and give and give again. Every time you come to the lodge meetings we will put the plate under your nose. We will call upon you to pay levies for new branches to be started in Timbuktu and in Tibet. We will ask you to give your leisure and your time to the work of the Union wherever you are, and in return we will give you nothing but the satisfaction of serving your fellow-men." I wonder would that Union get a very large number of members? I wonder would it get a very much larger number of members than the Church has succeeded in doing, and would it succeed in attaining to a very much closer unity than the Church has done? You see, the Church is an attempt to found a Union of pure unselfishness, whose members seek nothing and gain nothing but added power to serve their fellows.

'The world is full of selfish unions, it always has been full of them, but they are not any real advance; they are after all very little more than herds—herds and not societies. But the world will never be saved by herds, it will never be saved by selfish unions, it can only be saved by a union of service. I do not deny that there is an element of unselfishness in the working class movement. I do not in the least deny the sacrifices that men have willingly made to help their comrades in time of trouble, in strikes and lockouts, but I dare not trust overmuch to that. There is something very splendid about it, but it is not reliable. It is very largely the result of the knowledge that men are all in one boat, dependent upon one another for safety, and bound together by their fierce opposition to the enemy. It is a unity of spirit that is based rather upon force and fear than upon faith and hope, and the unity of spirit which is based upon force and fear does not, and cannot, last. We must attain to a higher unity than that if we are to save the world.

'The unity of your Unions is far too much akin to the unity of nations in time of war, and that is the least satisfactory and reliable kind of unity that I know anything of. There I think lies your chief difficulty. The Labour Party as yet has never been a Government, it has always been an Opposition, and it is always far easier to maintain loyalty and unity in an Opposition than it is in a Government. It is also of course far easier to be an Opposition than to be a Government. Being an Opposition is in some ways as easy as instructing the Commander-in-Chief how to win the Battle of the Somme with matches for armies round a glass of beer on a pub table; anybody can do it. Opposition is as much easier than Government as preaching is easier than practice, and believe me, I know something about the difference between those two. The real test of your movement will never come until it is called upon to form a Government. When that happens, I believe you will find your unity very much more difficult to maintain. You see, men possess all sorts of queer powers, but no power they possess is quite so bewildering as their power of self-deception. Men will honestly believe and earnestly argue to prove that their opinions are founded upon and their actions guided by principle, and that their policy is a reasonable one, when really there only lies behind it prejudice and self-interest.

'Although I do not believe that men are altogether determined by prejudice and interest, and still less that they need be altogether determined by those powers, still when I hear men arguing and bringing forward elaborate reasons for their opinions, I cannot help perceiving that the battle of reason is on the surface and the battle of prejudice and interest underneath. When the property owner argues with the proletarian, however reasonable each may be on the surface, one cannot help feeling that it is not his reason which makes him conservative and adds fire to his faith, but his property; and it is not reason which dyes the flag of the proletarian red, but the barren greyness of his life and his surroundings. It is comparatively easy to attain unity between all the "haves" in order to keep what they have, or between the "have nots" in order to gain what they have not—it is quite easy and also quite worthless. It is supremely difficult to make a unity between the "haves" and the "have nots," in order that they may help one another—it is extremely difficult, but is the one thing that is worth while. Sometimes you find people who belong to the "haves" joining with the "have nots," and you think you have attained something of the unity you desire, but if you investigate you find it is merely a matter of peculiar temperament. It is not really founded upon principle or upon reason, but upon some private prejudice. You have not really got away from the unity of the herd, you have not really attained the unity of the Society. So long as the members of a Society are all either interest-determined or temperament-determined people, real social unity is unattainable. Something must be found which will lift people above their interests and above their temperaments, and set them standing on the rock of principles.

'That is what the Church is seeking to do. That she does not altogether succeed in doing it I am free to confess. Her own splits and sections arise far more out of a conflict of interests and temperaments than from a conflict of real principles. Protestants are mostly Protestant out of the instinct of pugnacity, and Catholics are very largely Catholics for the same reason. Religious differences are enormously differences of prejudice rather than of judgment. I do not claim that we succeed in doing it, but I do claim that we have in us the seeds of success and some promise of it. Christianity has proved that men can become —and that quite humble and uneducated men can become—neither interest-determined nor temperament-determined, but God-determined people, and that is exactly what is needed. That is the only unity that will finally last and work, a unity which finds its centre somewhere above prejudice and above self-interest; but in order to attain that something more than abstract principles is needed, something more even than good laws is needed. Neither principle nor law has in it the power to secure obedience, power to determine what men shall think and do. Reason has no real chance when it has to do battle alone with passion, interest, and prejudice; only a greater passion can lift men out of the strife of tongues, the clash of unreasoning hopes and fears and hates and loves, and set them in the peace and security of a policy based upon principle.

'That is why Jesus of Nazareth, who knew man and needed not that any should tell Him what was in man, said that the first and great command was, "Thou shalt love the Lord thy God with all thy heart, with all thy mind, with all thy soul, and with all thy strength," and that then and only then was it worth loving your neighbour as yourself— because then and only then would all men become your neighbours, and establish a claim upon you apart from the fact of self-interest or natural likes and dislikes.

'There is an awful lot of talk among your people about loving your neighbours and being comrades, and it is quite sincere; but it is neither deep enough nor strong enough to lift them up above themselves in any real sense. It still means not so much that they love their neighbour as they love themselves, as that they love themselves in their neighbours. And that is why although the unity of your movement is impressive on the surface, I am not much impressed by its real value—it is really a unity of interest and very little else. I think, in fact I feel sure, that you have many troubles on ahead, and more troubles now than you are willing publicly to acknowledge. There are a great number of questions which at present do not bring you to the breaking point, because it is manifestly the best policy not to let them do so while you have a common enemy to conquer, and a common danger to avoid. Without denying the unselfishness that has been shown by working people to one another, I think it is true to say that your unity is a selfish unity, and therefore has not in it the power which can save the world.'

Humanity is the workers' God: they do not need a Christ.

Mr. O. L. 'Well, there is a lot of truth in that. Any one who knows anything at all about the inner workings of the Labour Movement knows that we are up against snags—and big snags. Again and again it has looked as though we were going to split upon the question of direct action and of compulsory communism, and there is of course—since we are in the house of truth—a continual strife between the principles of Craft

Unions and Trade Unions, and a good deal of friction among Unions themselves. But up to now we have managed to weather all these storms a good deal better, as it seems to me, than you have weathered yours. Although we have been threatened with splits again and again we have never actually split. There is no gulf among us so deep as the gulf which actually exists between Protestants and Catholics. Furthermore, I would deny that our basis of unity is a selfish one. It is very largely the love of humanity which unites us; we do feel that we are fighting the battle of the down-trodden and oppressed all the world over, and that we are knit together by a common love of the human race. We don't profess to know anything about God, but we do profess to know something about humanity, and a common enthusiasm for the uplift of the human race seems to me to be a much more natural and a much more real power for the purpose of lifting men above their interests and prejudices than the love of God can ever be. And so, in spite of what you say, I still think there is more chance of making a united world through Labour as a world movement than through the agency of your conflicting and intensely national churches.

'After all, there is a very real bond of unity between the workers of Britain and the workers of Russia, between the workers of the East and those of the West. "One touch of nature makes the whole world kin," and the working-class woman in Camberwell who has to go short is bound by a very real tie to her dusky sister in Calcutta. They are bound together there where they are divided on the question of religious faith, and we Labour people do recognise that no Union short of a world-wide Union is going to serve our purpose in the end.

We believe we can make the Chinaman and the Indian a good Trade Unionist long before you can get him to be a Christian at all, never mind a good one. The prospects of building up a brotherhood of man upon the common need of bread and butter seem to be far better than the prospects of building it on the love of God.'

Mr. O. C. 'I agree. They do seem much better, but are they really? Would it be a real brotherhood? Would it hold and stand the test of time? Would it mean very much more than the substitution of class wars for national wars? Mind you, I am not saying that it is not needed. The International bread-and-butter brotherhood is essential—it is needed—but is it all that is needed? Would it not still be a selfish unity which could only last as long as it had a common interest to bind it and a common enemy to fight?

'The real question is as to whether the love of humanity is or can be made strong enough to overcome self-interest, national prejudice, colour prejudice, and to bridge over the thousand gulfs which divide men into sections.

'After all, does it not finally mean that you still believe men to be in the main economically determined and inevitably so? Does it not mean that you believe that men's real God is and must be a God of Gold, and that to secure what you would call a just and equitable distribution of that God's favours is all that is needed to secure human peace?

'It seems to me that here again we are back upon our old question of economic determinism, and I do not believe that that determinism is now or ever can be made complete, or that if it ever was made complete it could issue in anything but continued and intensified struggles and strife. Experience goes to show that the human demand for material joys is literally insatiable, that the more a man has the more he wants. Your bread-and-butter brotherhood would inevitably tend to become a struggle for an impossible standard of life, as luxuries came to be regarded as universal necessities, a process which is actually going on. That is the question which it seems to me your movement has never squarely faced. Are you out for an international class unity, or are you out for an international brotherhood including all classes ?

'Of course, it is fairly evident that even on the bread-and-butter level a world-wide Union is essential. It is no use struggling for a better standard of life, higher wages, and shorter hours in Britain, while other nations continue to work long hours for low wages. Even on the purely economic level every national question is an international one. What are the facts of the case?

'"We have a population of about fifty million souls crowded on to a few square miles. We are the most highly artificial community that the world has ever known. We have, it is true, certain natural advantages the chief of which is an ample supply of good coal. We have a good climate, a good soil, and energetic and capable people, and a certain amount of accumulated capital here and abroad; but we cannot even keep ourselves alive for more than a few months unless we sell to the rest of the world, at prices at which they can buy them, such raw materials as we can export, and the many manufactured articles for the making of which we depend upon the co-operation of Capital and Labour, on the organising ability of the employers and the skill of the employed. In order to live, in fact, we have got to work at least as hard and as skilfully as our competitors."

'Those are the facts of the case on the bread-and-butter level alone; and while it is true that up to a certain point you can reduce hours and increase output, that is not equally true of all industries, and is not true at all of some. Beyond a certain point in any industry the shortening of hours is bound to affect output, and an increase in the standard of wages is bound to increase the cost of production, and therefore make it impossible for us working short hours at high wages to sell our goods in competition with other nations working long hours for low wages. Superior efficiency of organisation would have some effect in neutralising our disadvantage, but could not possibly abolish it altogether. It is therefore perfectly plain that whatever advantage we win for ourselves we must at the same time strive to get for others. Even on the bread-and-butter level international co-operation is therefore a necessity. But the point is as to whether it is attainable on that level. I do not think it is. At best international class unity can only issue in world-wide class wars, and at worst it may prove a dismal failure and issue in nothing.

'The supposition that seems to me to underlie the hope men have of attaining human peace by methods of class unity appears to be that classes are entirely artificial and that it is possible to secure a world in which there shall be no classes at all. That supposition is, I hold, essentially false. It is not true that what are called the " upper classes " are only upper through luck, inheritance, or fraud. They are upper partly through essential superiority of brain power and ability. While classes are at present indeed largely artificial, there are natural classes springing out of natural inequalities. There is no lie more utterly devoid of truth than the lie of the equality of man. Men are not equal and cannot be made equal by any power in heaven or earth. There are, and there always will be, enormous natural inequalities among men in respect of strength of body and brain power. When you raise men above the bread-and-butter level, and teach them to love God and man; then you can get them to see what human inequality means—get them to see that superior ability is God's call to service, that strength is a summons to protect the weak. That is the Truth which Christ can make men see, but so long as you are down upon the bread-and-butter level, and men of unequal ability and unequal brain power, and nations of unequal development and unequal natural advantages, are mainly determined economically, class wars and class domination will prove to be perpetual necessities. There is not and there cannot be any escape from them while you remain down on the bread-and-butter level.

' And so it seems to me that for the

purpose of world-wide unity, which we both perceive to be absolutely necessary, unless international competition is to bring the standard of life of the workers down to the lowest level, we must find some basis of unity higher than bread and butter, and what is that basis to be? Apparently you would say that it is to be a common love of humanity, which you hold is a natural thing, one touch of nature making the whole world kin; but that is a dismal fallacy. It is much truer to say that one touch of nature makes the whole world cats — spitting, scratching, and clawing cats. The touch of nature only makes the whole world kin as long as there is nothing to make them anything else, but it is not natural for men to love one another, it is much more natural for them to fight herd against herd. The love of humanity, when it does not stand for the common need of bread and butter as a unifying power, stands naturally for little more than a rather vague and sentimental aspiration. If it is to become anything like strong enough to do battle with the passions and prejudices that cleave and divide men from one another, it must be raised to the Nth power—it must become a religion, and, if I may say so, something of a fanatical religion at that. Only so can it be anything like strong enough really to determine men's thoughts and actions.

'Of course, the love of God and the love of men are not real alternatives. In Christianity there is no " either " and " or " between those two, it is a question of " both," " and." Christianity is a passion for God in man, for God Incarnate —a passion for Jesus Christ. Our claim is that in Jesus redeemed humanity can become so supreme reality as to dominate and sway the whole of a man's life. To love humanity as it is with all its cruelties, its meanness, its stupidities, and baseness, is to tax any sane man's powers of sentimentality beyond bearing; but humanity as seen in Christ, cleansed and redeemed, can and does become the ruling passion of a man's life; and it is that possibility, and that possibility alone, that gives me hope of attaining to anything like a real brotherhood of man.'

Mr. O. L. 'Well, it seems to me to be an extraordinarily slender hope. I acknowledge the difficulties that face us in the effort to attain brotherhood on the bread-and-butter level, but it seems to me to be at any rate the next step. When we have attained to an international bread-and-butter brotherhood of the working classes, I think we may find it much easier—and you may find it much easier—to bring this higher spiritual motive into play, but meanwhile it seems to be of more practical use to concentrate upon world-wide working-class solidarity.'

Mr. O. C. ' I cannot agree. It seems to me that, so far from being easier if you attain your object, it will in some ways become harder, and that in attaining your lower object you may very well make the higher one impossible. If you continually strive to unite men on the bread-and-butter level and with the bread-and-butter plea, you continually tend to deaden their minds and harden their hearts to any higher appeal. And, moreover, you do not really decide upon the vastly important question as to what your next unit of co-operation is. Is it to be the class or the nation ? In striving to make united classes you tend to make divided nations, and that is one of my great criticisms of your present policy.

' What are you really out for ? Are you really out for the League of Nations ?

That is, do you really want to make a united British nation with a social conscience that regulates its actions, and make it the leading member of a League of Nations whose actions are governed and controlled by a common social conscience? Or are you out for the class-conscious workers' unity in this and every other nation of the world, because the two things really do tend to cut one another out? You people are always talking about nationalising this, that, and the other, thus taking the nation as your unit of co-operation, while your practical policy tends to make national unity difficult, if not impossible.

'You cannot get a national unity on a basis of exasperated class antagonism. I know, and I think the Church knows, precisely what we want in that matter —we want a League of Nations, acting with the common Christian conscience. We definitely want national unity as a step to international unity, and we are all out for the League of Nations. It seems to us that your support of the League of Nations is very lukewarm, and that you constitute one of the main obstacles to its success; because in order to have a League of Nations we must have nations to league, and you seem to be constantly trying to split the nation upon economic issues, and jeering at patriotism as a hypocritical disguise for Capitalist ambition and militarism.'

The Church worships a National God.

Mr. O. L. 'Well and aren't we justified in that? Hasn't patriotism been the curse of the world—isn't it the curse of the world to-day? My country right or wrong. Has it not roused men's worst passions and led them to do some of their vilest deeds? Can the nation ever be anything else but a militarist conception, only tending to expand into a larger and more deadly curse, the curse of militarist imperialism? Surely we workers have suffered enough from national hatred and national ambition and imperialistic jingoism to make us fear and distrust nationalism, militarism, and patriotism, and all the other rotten isms of the same sort?

'That is one of my great grouses against you and your Church. You have given and still give your blessing to the eyewash and cant of militarist nationalism. You bless colours, say prayers over guns, give the proudest place in your churches to war memorials, and talk and teach to children the petty, puerile, and flag-waving patriotism which makes pride in the fact that we have painted the better part of the world's map red a virtue, whereas to us it seems to be a cause for shame. We have painted it red—a very significant colour—and for us working people it not only glares, but stinks, stinks with the stench of battle-fields, the dry, parched, sickening smell that calls up memories of an August day in the valley of the Somme. Can patriotism ever be redeemed, and can the nations of the Empire ever be anything but a menace to the welfare of the workers of the world ? '

Mr. O. C. ' I see and I sympathise down to the ground, but nevertheless I do believe that patriotism can and must be redeemed, and that imperialism can and must be made a pure and noble thing. The nation has, and ought to have, in it the possibility of unity not only for war but for peace. There can be and must be a patriotism based not upon our common hatred of other nations but upon our common love of our own. I find such a patriotism very much alive in my own soul and in that of others. I love the English land, its mountains and hills, its rivers and dells, its great cities and the roaring traffic of their streets, and this love is not merely a sentiment, it is something with a tremendous hold on the very depths of my nature. It is in the deepest sense natural, and would move me to action and to sacrifice instinctively, and I believe it exists in hundreds of thousands of ordinary men, and even now has power to move them to their very depths.

'Hitherto it has exercised its greatest power as the motive calling to war, but I believe it can, when touched by the love of God, move men to sacrifice in the cause of peace. It only needs what I believe to be perfectly possible, that the love which we have for our own land should quicken us to sympathy with the love that others have of theirs, that we should recognise clearly that what the countryside of England is to Englishmen, the rolling downs of France are to the French, and so all the world over, that we should learn because of our patriotism to respect the patriotism of others and to look at questions from their point of view.

'The nation does seem to me to present the next natural unit of co-operation. It provides a basis of unity which is not temporal and purely material, but is eternal, and can be made essentially spiritual. I am as much against militarist patriotism as ever you can be, and so I believe are Christians as a whole; but I believe that patriotism is essentially Christian. I find running through the whole teaching of Jesus like a refrain the love of His own people and the longing that they should play a part in the world worthy of the call that God had given them. I believe that Jesus of Nazareth put before the leaders of the Jewish nation a perfectly definite and clear-cut proposal for the working out of their national destiny. A fierce and passionate patriotism had always been a characteristic of the Jew. Jesus never sought to destroy that patriotism, He sought to purify and uplift it. He called the nation to leave behind all their militarist dreams, all the patriotism of conquest, and all hopes of a miraculous interference by God to crush their enemies. He called them from a militarist, superstitious, and material patriotism to a spiritual and moral one. He held up to them their national destiny as a career not of conquest and tyranny but of service and leadership. He sought to unite His people upon a spiritual basis. One of the greatest sorrows of His life was that the nation could not hear. " Oh, if thou hadst known, even thou, in this thy day, the things which belong unto thy peace! but now are they hid from thine eyes." " O Jerusalem, Jerusalem, which killest the prophets, and stonest them that are sent unto thee; how often would I have gathered thy children together, as a hen doth gather her brood under her wings, and ye would not!" It is the cry of a patriot. He did seek to turn them from base and material patriotism, but He did not seek to turn them from patriotism altogether, and I do not believe that we are meant to turn from patriotism altogether. There is such a thing as a right and Christian patriotism, and in it lies the hope of a world-wide unity. Whereas class consciousness as a basis of unity seems to me to be artificial and temporary, national consciousness or patriotism seems to be natural and lasting. My great grouse against you is that you tend to put your class before your country, and in your endeavour to unite the class you tend to divide the nation. I am constantly finding at your meetings that you prefer singing the Red Flag to the National Anthem, and that not so much because you have any feeling against the King or the Monarchy as because you despise and dislike patriotism. Here I think lies one of your great weaknesses. You are halting between two opinions—two units of co-operation, the nation and the class—and by your hesitation you put a lot of good people off, who see the justice of your cause, but will not support you because they feel you are not patriots. The Duke of Northumberland's mad stunt about the whole Labour Movement being a vast conspiracy to destroy the British Empire is a gross and exaggerated version of a fear which haunts a number of level-headed men who feel in their bones that there is some truth in what he says. Why can't you make up your minds on this business? Why cannot you go whole-heartedly for the League of Nations, and loyally support the British Empire, which as a League in itself of free nations should form an essential part of the world's League? You are weakening yourselves by this hesitation. You do not seem to have any really constructive foreign policy at all. Is it to be the nation or the class, that is the question.'

The Workers are bitterly disappointed by the League of Nations.

Mr. O. L. 'Well, I'm willing to admit that is where we wobble, and that our wobbling is a great weakness, and is more likely to split us than almost anything else. A good number of the working people of England are Imperialists and believe in a British Empire, and moreover are very distinct patriots. That is one of the reasons why a number of good Trade Unionists fail to vote Labour at election time. But surely it is fairly obvious why we do not make the patriotic plea, support the British Empire and go in whole-heartedly for the League of Nations? You know as well as I do the amount of bunkum and eye-wash that surrounds those ideas. Patriotism, as I have said, is militarist to the core. It calls up all the idea of "My country against others." It is by the power of the patriotic plea that the Capitalists have again and again been able to drive the workers out to be butchered in their thousands, and to butcher their brothers too. And as for Imperialism, it seems to me to be even more essentially militarist. However much it may be disguised, it is founded upon pure force and surrounded with a perfect cloud of lies. It is supposed that the coloured peoples, whom we patronisingly call the subject races, have a kind of natural tendency to disappear before the advance of the superior white races. But we know, and you know, what the cause of that natural tendency is. It is not what that blustering German, von Treitschke, called " the basilisk glance" of essential superiority, it is simply the corruption of native peoples by the conscienceless exploitation of their ignorance for profit, the degradation of their physique through the sale of intoxicant liquors and drugs, the stealing of their land, sometimes blatant and open, and sometimes under cover of so-called legal procedure. The record of the white man's conduct to the weaker peoples is about as black as it can be. Imperialism has a disreputable history. The working people know all these facts or many of them, and they distrust Imperialism. As for the League of Nations, well, you know as well as I do that the bottom has fallen out of the whole thing. As it stands now it is only playing with the question. We are bitterly disappointed in it. We thought it really was going to lead to something, and it might have led to great things if private vested interests, and " business " here and in America, had not killed it before it was born, by utterly destroying its economic basis. A League of Nations which is simply a legal affair and has no economic basis is simply useless as a preventative of war. If after the Armistice we could have preserved and adapted for use in time of peace the international system of co-operative economic management which had arisen to meet the necessities of war, if it had not all broken down under the pressure of vested interests, anxious to get back as soon as possible to the competitive game of grab, we would have had some hope for the League. But to suppose that you can let the world go back to that game, and then keep the peace by setting up international courts of law, and holding Councils and Assemblies, which can discuss anything except the one thing that matters, seems to us to be nothing but nonsense, and hypocritical nonsense at that. It is, as Mr. Garvin remarks in his book, *The Economic Foundations of Peace,* like " trying to cure a man in a high fever by presenting him with a new suit of clothes." How can you hope to unite a world in a League of Nations when the nations that you seek to league are not from the economic standpoint units at all but mobs. It is as true to-day as it was before the war that the nations of the world are only nations when they meet their enemies in the gate, they are not nations when they meet their friends in the marketplace. And as long as that is so, and we continue to work on a competitive basis, there can be no real league. It is either international economic co-operation or the pre-war chaos issuing in another shambles. When industry can be nationalised, and nations which are real economic units can meet to consult

with other nations which are also
economic units, and can come to rational
and just decisions about their share of
the raw material of the world, then there
would be a prospect of some real League
of Nations. But to ask the working
people to put their trust in this hypocritical and hastily constructed addition to the purely militarist Treaty of
Versailles is to put too great a strain
altogether upon our powers of credulity.
We know too well what is going to
happen to it. It is going to be made a
tool of as the Holy Alliance was before
it. It is going to be just another instance of that which occurs again and
again in history, the fooling of the good
people of the world by the clever devils.
Unless international unity is founded
upon a basis of real economic co-operation between nations as economic units
it has not, and cannot have, any real
basis at all. We have been standing by

for the last two years, we Labour people, and watching all our hopes and dreams " go West " one by one under a continual political barrage from the vested interests backed by the Press which they control. We did hope that things were going to be worked upon a real co-operative basis. There was the skeleton of a co-operative economic system ready to hand, only needing to be clothed with flesh by practical application, and made alive by the spirit of goodwill. We thought that was going to take place, but all we have seen is the ruthless destruction of the skeleton itself, while the Capitalists do a sort of war dance over its remains, singing what they call a song of freedom and unfettered enterprise. We are not in a mood to believe in anything very much, and least of all are we in a mood to believe in a League of Nations, which is all up in the clouds and has no basis in reality.'

Mr. O. C. 'I see your difficulty, and I sympathise with you all the way. I too, and my fellow Christians, have watched with bitterness and dismay the destruction of our hopes by the reactionary spirit and by greed, but I would once more remind you of what we have clearly seen in previous discussions of economic questions, namely, that they are not the real root questions, but that underneath them lie spiritual and psychological issues. What is it that has destroyed this skeleton? You say that it is the treachery and greed of the Capitalists, and in saying that you allow that the real enemy is a spiritual enemy. Here, as in the other issues that we discussed, it is the spiritual factor which is the final and the real one. It is but little use doing what you and your people are so fond of doing, blaming Governments and Ministers, throwing the whole weight of responsibility upon your representatives at Paris and at Westminster. The truth of the matter is that we always get the Government that we deserve, and it is much more the ignorance and apathy of the peoples that is to blame than the greed and incompetence of their official representatives. I believe that the General Election of 1918 was one of the most shameful episodes in our history. The Prime Minister had then a magnificent opportunity. He only needed courage, and he could have called upon the people to give him a mandate to make a real peace. But would they have answered that call? The Prime Minister is a strange man and difficult to understand, but there is absolutely no denying his genius in one respect. No politician that ever lived has had a greater power of feeling the pulse of the people upon which his power depends. It took him a week or ten days to feel that pulse, and then he came out with his programme:

The Kaiser's head; the punishment of enemy war criminals; Germany to pay the whole cost of the war; Britain for the British, and the rehabilitation of those whom the war had broken. It was a mean and ignominious programme, but it was overwhelmingly and immediately popular. It was overwhelmingly and immediately popular with the working classes, and why? Because there was a wrong spirit abroad. The Prime Minister knew as only he could know the political possibilities and impossibilities of the situation, and he got his reward—a thumping big machine majority capable of crushing all opponents—but who is to blame for that?'

Mr. O. L. 'Who is to blame? Why, you. You are supposed to be the spiritual leaders, aren't you? Why the devil didn't you lead? Where was your Christ then? Why didn't your Church speak, and speak out? Why didn't she defy the politicians and give us a real lead ? If in any sense she is the national Church and represents the nation, why didn't she give the people the lead for which they craved ?'

Mr. O. C. 'She did, as far as ever she was able. In the babel of voices that arose I contend that her voice was always on the right side. As far as ever her power to do so went she did lead the people. The Report of the Lambeth Conference upon International affairs sums up the message which was then given from thousands of pulpits in the land. Many of us wore ourselves out in trying to bring that message home, but we found that it fell very largely upon deaf ears. We were not taken seriously. I contend that we gave the lead but there was no following, and I contend that there was no following because of the ghastly gulf that separates Organised Labour from Organised Christianity. If we could have spoken together upon this question, together and with one voice—insisting upon the utter necessity of a new national and international order—I believe we could have made it far more possible for those who had the welfare of the world at heart in Paris to make some sort of a real stand. But your people were blind to the importance of the moral issue at stake, and our voice was too weak to carry any distance in such an uproar. We have failed, but that failure which we both share, for I am not denying that in part the Church did fail and fall short of its duty, ought surely to warn us of the need, the essential need, we have of one another, of how Christ's Church needs you to give her body, and you need her to give you soul. Surely you ought to be able to see that it is madness to neglect the force of the religious motive in a time of pressing need like this—for mind you the time is short—the next two or three years will probably settle for good or evil the question of the better order, national and international.

'"If the nations settle down into acquiescence with oppression and corruption, if the disillusionment and cynical disbelief of the present become the permanent atmosphere of the world, then we will drift into confusion, and it will take another great war to rouse us, and that great war will inevitably come unless we act now."

'It is imperative that you should see that the final impossibilities of this situation, if there are any, are moral and spiritual impossibilities, and can only be overcome by a moral and spiritual effort. I am sure that that moral and spiritual effort must be made in the first place by us as a nation, and that what we have to set ourselves to do is to create the new patriotism which is filled, not with the spirit of commerce, nor with the spirit of war, but with the spirit of Christ.

P

Now if we as a Church try to spread abroad that spirit of regenerated patriotism and to create a new national unity, we are bound to find in you as you are at present, not a powerful ally but a powerful foe. Your practical policy and your class propaganda, based as it is upon the impossible materialism of Marx, is tending to split and break up the nation into warring factions. You talk a great deal about the nationalisation of industry, but I tell you that any statesman who tried to work industry on a national scale with the spiritual tone of the people as it is to-day, with as little love of the nation among the people, and as little sense of the nation as a unit of co-operation as there is now among all classes, would be little short of a lunatic. It is not only the commercial classes who have undergone an unreasonable reaction from a blind and militarist patriotism to a mean and sectional selfishness—the same spirit is abroad among your people. Is there any guarantee whatever that if the nation did take over any of the great staple industries the workpeople would then be loyal? Have we any reason for supposing that the patriotic motive for work is any stronger among your rank and file than it is among the Capitalist and employing classes? I am bound to confess that I see no reason for supposing anything of the kind. But I do believe that there are a large number of men of all classes who at present are silent and bewildered, who would become vocal and powerful as members of a thoroughly Christianised Labour Movement. It is to this body that I look to pull the nation together and turn its face once more to the task which is its manifest destiny—the task of building up the new national and international economic order. The present mad reaction cannot last, we must swing back to sanity sooner or later, and we must make it sooner or it may be too late. We want—we must have—the new patriotism, and that is why you must come out with a really constructive policy. I feel with you the weakness of the League of Nations as it is at present. I see in it many glaring faults besides those that you have mentioned, and have watched with bitterness and disgust the corruption of the Mandatory System into a series of annexations for purposes of economic exploitation, and the abuse by the great Powers of what the Covenant unctuously calls " the sacred trust of civilisation." I cannot help feeling that many of the statesmen signed the Covenant with their tongues in their cheeks, and never really meant to make any sacrifice to carry out its provisions. I see plainly that it was run through in the teeth of the deadest kind of apathy, breaking out

THE DOG COLLAR

at intervals into the fiercest opposition. It is a poor thing, a very poor thing, as long as America, Russia, and Germany are out of it, but I contend that it is all that we have got, the only real fruit of victory that we possess. And, poor as it is, I believe that it can become an enormously powerful instrument for good if only your body and mine together put their whole force behind it, perceiving clearly and holding firmly to the fact that the impossibilities that we are called upon to overcome are spiritual impossibilities arising out of the greed and apathy of the peoples. That is the truth we must hold on to. The great difficulties are at bottom moral and spiritual difficulties, and it is out of those that the economic difficulties arise. All the Covenant does, all it could do in the nature of things, is to provide the political machinery necessary for dealing with the new world that has grown up during the century of mechanical power. It provides the political machinery, but it cannot work it. The power to work it must come not from the brain or the hand, but from the spirit of mankind. The physical unity of the world is an accomplished fact. God has actually brought that to pass over our heads and without our realising what was taking place. By the gift of mechanical power which He has given us through inspired inventors and scientific discoverers, God has unified the world physically. The nations have been married by the act of God—they have been forced to take one another on " for better, for worse, for richer, for poorer, in sickness and in health," and there is no death to part them, and not even Lord Buckmaster can get them a divorce. Those whom God hath joined together no man *can* put asunder. The world is one now in body. It was supposed before the war that this physical unity and complete economic interdependence of the nations would of itself bring peace. Books were written to show that inasmuch as we were absolutely dependent upon one another we could not fight. We could not fight because it would be suicidal madness. It is suicidal madness, and yet we have fought, are fighting, and we shall fight again, unless we can build up a spiritual unity, corresponding to the physical unity that has been built. We have been married, put into one house, made dependent upon one another, but marriage does not of itself create domestic bliss. Two people often live in peace and amity until they marry, and then quarrel for the rest of their lives. Many marriages begin at the altar and end in the police court, with a charge of assault and battery. When a man's married his troubles begin—but by the help of God it may be the beginning of the end

—only by the help of God, the Spirit of self-sacrifice and love. True marriages are made in heaven, they can only be made in heaven. The mistake is to suppose that they can be made on earth. The Covenant of the League of Nations is their marriage certificate—the real sign of their interdependence—but it may end as thousands of sordid marriages do end, in utter ruin, unless the spirit of unity turns interdependence into co-operation. The problem is a spiritual problem, and the difficulties are at bottom spiritual difficulties. We must perceive that truth clearly and get to grips with it promptly. If we do not perceive the spiritual reality behind economic problems, we shall not solve them, and if we do not solve them they will dissolve us. The situation is critical and the time is short. Industrial decay is a present fact, and the root causes of it are spiritual and international.

'It is perfectly clear that we can only live as we sell our goods abroad at prices at which the people of other nations can buy them. It is perfectly true that it is impossible for the individual employer here at home to keep his works running and his people employed when they demand short hours, high wages, and do slack work, while he has to compete in the competitive markets of the world with peoples who are working long hours for low wages, and working hard. We have got to come to an international arrangement about hours of labour, and in the end about wages. The Covenant of the League of Nations has perceived this, and has made a very real effort to grapple with the question, an effort which I believe to be entirely on the right lines. The Washington Conference appears to me to have been one of the most hopeful experiments that has ever been made, and if the Labour people of the world would back it up for all they are worth, I believe that great things would come out of it. The International Labour Organisation of the League of Nations appears to me to be sane and practical, only needing the backing of the peoples, the backing which we, united into one body, or at any rate operating in friendly and hearty co-operation, could give it. It is necessary that we perceive perfectly clearly that it is useless our trying to raise the standard of living among our own people unless we at the same time take steps to raise it among the people of the world, and I do not see any other method by which that can be done except through the League of Nations. The attempt to do it on the class warfare basis through Workers' Internationals can, I am convinced, only ruin our power of production by perpetuating through the whole world-field of industry the squabble over the product. I see clearly before us two immediate steps. First of all, we must promote the unity of the nation and then promote the unity of the world through a league of united nations. That is our programme, and I think it ought to be yours, but from what I can make out of your present practical policy, and the theory which lies behind many of your speeches, it certainly is not your programme; in fact, you don't seem to me to have any definitely constructive foreign policy whatever.'

Wanted a real Labour Leader

Mr. O. L. 'Well, I don't know that we have. There are many of us who are troubled in our minds, and seriously troubled, for that very reason. Somehow we don't seem to have any great constructive force in the House of Commons or in the country. The criticisms of the Government in the House of Commons by our party we feel are generally entirely just but rarely practical and helpful, and I think you are right in saying that our weakness lies in the fact that we have not yet made up our minds as to whether class or the nation is to be the next unit of co-operation. But if you are so jolly sure that it ought to be the nation, why the blazes don't you get a move on? What feeds us up about you is that you are so much up in the air. You are always laying down great principles and never building anything on them. Take this Lambeth Conference Report that you are all so cock-a-whoop about, what does that amount to? To us it seems only to mean that for the first time probably in the history of the world a bench of Christian bishops has talked common sense. Of course, to you that may seem to be something in the nature of a miracle—a kind of answer to the prayer that the God who alone works great marvels would send down upon His bishops and curates the healthful spirit of His grace, but you can't expect us to be very excited about it, and when it comes to the point, it always seems to me that you shirk the issue. You seem to us to be shirking what is the greatest question of to-day, the question as to whether the communities have or can have souls, and whether nations can be held responsible for their actions as nations. During the war your Christian pulpits rang with the doctrine of national responsibility, and you explicitly taught that Germany could be held responsible as a nation and could be talked to as a nation about the crimes she had committed—about her Belgian atrocities and all the rest of it. If that is so, then surely we as a nation can be held responsible, and can be talked to about our atrocities, our Whitechapel and Sheffield and Manchester atrocities, and our South African and Indian ones, and our Irish ones too. You Christians appear to us to be still individualists, content with teaching men their individual duty, and laying down the principles that ought to govern their individual lives, but you are too weak and too cowardly to attack the question of the national conscience, and the principles that ought to govern our national action.'

Mr. O. C. 'Well, as a matter of fact the root of the matter does lie and always must lie with the individual, but it is not our wish, and I say that our recent attitude shows that it is not our wish, that the matter should rest there. We as a Church are intensely anxious to form a national conscience, and it is because we are so anxious to do this that many of us desire to effect some measure of practical co-operation with your body. We do not in the least underrate the importance of the material issues at

THE DOG COLLAR

stake. We perceive, and have recently shown that we perceive, the intense importance of good housing and a decent standard of human life. We do not underrate the importance of the material issues, but we say that you do underrate the importance of the spiritual issues, and that your policy is merely destructive and not constructive, precisely because you are blind to the importance of the spiritual side; precisely because you ridiculously underestimate the power of the spiritual and moral motive over mankind. The issue that we want to put before you is simply this, that while a Labour Movement based upon sound moral and religious principles, and taking full advantage of the power of the moral and religious appeal, may very well prove the salvation of the world, a Labour Movement which looks upon economic questions as purely economic questions, and which has nothing but a very dim perception of the deeper spiritual issues, can only plunge the world into a more desperate confusion. There is an urgent and growing need for a moral revival, and it is to promote that, to get it going, and to give it organised power, that we seek your aid. Furthermore, we believe that unless you adopt that course you will not even succeed in bettering the standard of life among our people. It comes back to this, that if you will not have the Kingdom of Heaven you cannot have the kingdom of earth. If you will not seek first the Kingdom of God and His righteousness, then all those material things can never be added unto you. There lies and always has lain the choice; you must either have Christ or a continuance of this appalling muddle.'

Mr. O. L. 'Well, I'm not going to deny the need of a moral revival. The most thoughtful of our leaders have said

THE DOG COLLAR 241

very much the same thing to me before now many a time. I think it is needed, and I think it is needed among our people too, but what I am doubtful is as to whether you Christians, even if we backed you up, could bring it about. You will need to rid your Christ of a tremendous lot of barbed-wire entanglements that surround Him now. You will need to state far more clearly what it is you believe, and how it applies to the world of to-day. You will need to explain how it is that the Church, for which in the past you have made such exaggerated and ridiculous claims as a divinely ordained and divinely guided society, has made in the past so many egregious blunders, and been responsible for so many grievous wrongs. Jesus of Nazareth is all right, but to the workers it seems almost as true to say that the Christian churches are all wrong, and have been wrong for centuries. When you claim for the Church divine guidance and a divine foundation, and we look for signs following, they seem to be far to seek. When you priests claim for yourselves divine ordination and divine authority, and we look for signs of confirmation, they seem to be remarkable for their absence. Divine ordination does not seem to make you wiser or more intelligent. You seem to us very much like other men, only not so human and very often not so generous and so charitable. We cannot believe in the institution unless you give us the men. A divine Church ought to give us divine men, and it does not, it only gives us men that are divines, quarrelsome and narrow-minded divines. Give us leaders and we might follow.'

Mr. O. C. 'That is always your cry. I wonder how far it is sincere. You continually shift the moral responsibility. You grouse at the Church as it is. Do you ever consider what you might make of it if you were loyal members of it? Priests may be poor people, they often are. The Church has only the laity to choose from, and they are a poor lot, and a very selfish lot, and the priesthood is poorly paid. Business, and even political agitation, is a much more paying game. It is easy to say that the Church only gives you quarrelsome divines, but is it true? I know scores of parish priests who labour like blacks in filthy places, beggaring themselves and their families to serve and help the people of this land. Parsons as a class may be failures, all sorts of people as a class are failures. Politicians, school teachers, Labour leaders, doctors as classes are failures, human beings as a class are failures, but in each class there are some signs of success, is some glimmer of the Spirit—something of God. We are not asking you to follow parsons, or trust in the

Church as it is. We are asking you to follow God and have faith in the Church as it is to be. You cry out for a leader, a human leader who shall issue a compelling call, and supply infallible guidance. Well, he will never come. The lead has been given, the leader is here. Christ is the leader, the only leader of this Western world. If you will accept Christ as God, you will find a leader who will never fail. Supposing your members instead of confining their social work to attendance at political meetings, and getting up agitations, were to sacrifice some of their leisure and pleasure to the work of teaching and guiding our young people and children to be real Christians. Supposing that in every parish in the land Labour Organisations backed the Church, not so much with money as with work. There in the churches is the educational plant you need—there is the great opportunity.

Nothing that could happen in this country would so help the cause of righteousness and justice as that every parson in the land should wake some Sunday morning and go into his church and find it cram full of Trade Unionists. He would preach a different sermon that morning, and a better one still in the evening. Wonderful things would become possible in the parish. Drunkenness could be crushed out easily. Sensuality and sordid waste of money would cease. Ragged children could be clothed and hungry children fed. It would be the beginning of the Brotherhood. And you would be surprised how different the parson would become. I tell you this, nine out of every ten parsons *start* as the best fellows in the world, the very best, full of generous enthusiasm and desire to do good. They start well, but the job kills them, because of the deadweight of apathy among the peoples.

People fight shy of the parson, and he gets out of touch—but is that *all* his fault—is it not partly yours ? Do your members, do your leaders try to know him and to back him ? If you did you would see wonders often. I am certain that this country could be even now transformed economically, politically, and socially in a single generation, if the whole rank and file of the Labour Movement became genuinely and honestly Christian—set to work themselves to train and educate their children as Christians, not leaving it to the parson and the professional teacher, but doing it *themselves*. We have the plant and there is amongst us —crucified indeed and struggling, but present—the *Spirit*, the spirit of Christ which is God. It only needs you—the great Organised body of Labour—and we could bring about the great revolution in a single generation—without one drop of blood. Won't you come ? '

Mr. O. L. 'Would you have us? Wouldn't you boss us or try to? Wouldn't you try to tame us and keep us quiet? Don't you want us rather to swell your congregations than to save our souls?'

Mr. O. C. 'No, we don't. Honour bright we don't. I'm not only speaking for myself, I'm speaking for ninety per cent. of the parsons. We want you for Christ's sake and your own. The lead has been given. God is the leader. Couldn't you follow?'

'So long!' How long?

Mr. O. L. 'I don't know. I'm afraid our fellows will never listen. But they might, maybe, in time. There's something in it any way. I hope we shall meet again. Until then—So long!'

Mr. O. C. 'So long!'

(He turns and goes out, saying to himself) 'How long?—My God, how long? There's that house I was in last night. A pig-stye. Man drunk—woman syphilitic—children consumptive—and it need not be—it need not be. I can hear the woman's voice now, " Come in out of that you —— little ——," and it could all be changed—by Christ—in one generation. Dear God, why should men be so stupid and so blind ? '

UNIVERSITY OF CALIFORNIA, LOS ANGELES
THE UNIVERSITY LIBRARY
This book is DUE on the last date stamped below

OCT 2 1945

JAN 8 - 1952
JAN 8 RECD

JAN 8 1952

JAN 1 8 1981

MAR 2 9 1981

JUN 1 5 1986

UNIV. OF CALIFORNIA
AT
LOS ANGELES

HD
6338
S93d

ImTheStory.com

Personalized Classic Books in many genre's

Unique gift for kids, partners, friends, colleagues

Customize:
- Character Names
- Upload your own front/back cover images (optional)
- Inscribe a personal message/dedication on the inside page (optional)

Customize many titles Including
- Alice in Wonderland
- Romeo and Juliet
- The Wizard of Oz
- A Christmas Carol
- Dracula
- Dr. Jekyll & Mr. Hyde
- And more...

Emily's Adventures In Wonderland

Ryan & Julia